55 CELEBRATION
DOUGHCRAFT
—— DESIGNS ——

55 CELEBRATION
DOUGHCRAFT
— DESIGNS —

LINDA ROGERS

David & Charles

For my family Ken, Kate and Emma

Information on ready made doughcraft sculptures is
available from Linda Rogers, 'Dough Designs', The Old
School, Gretton Road, Gotherington, Cheltenham,
Gloucestershire GL52 4EP. It is an infringement of the law
of copyright to copy these designs for commercial purposes.

A D A V I D & C H A R L E S B O O K

First published in the UK in 1996

Text and designs Copyright © Linda Rogers 1996
Photography and layout Copyright ©
David & Charles 1996

A catalogue record for this book is
available from the British Library.

ISBN 0 7153 0389 9

Photography by Paul Biddle
Illustrations by Lorraine Harrison
Book design by The Bridgewater Book Company Limited
Typeset/Page make-up by Lee Forster
and printed in Great Britain
by Butler & Tanner Ltd
for David & Charles
Brunel House Newton Abbot Devon

✳ Contents ✳

✳ *Introduction* ✳

*W*elcome to the art of doughcraft! The most wonderful thing about this hobby is that anybody can do it. However lacking in artistic ability you think you are, you can be guaranteed to produce a perfectly respectable result. Some of the more complicated designs in this book may take a little longer to master, but bearing this in mind, each special occasion catered for offers a choice of project. There is a simple easy-to-follow design for the uninitiated, many of which are also suitable for children to make, and a more complicated project for the experienced or brave among you!

A piece of doughcraft makes a wonderful gift, and indeed much of its history is associated with giving. The ancient civilisations of Greece and Egypt used it to make offerings to their gods and an old German legend tells that a gift of 'Salzteig' as it is known brings good luck and prosperity to the recipient. Everybody appreciates a present that has been made especially for them and this book offers a choice of over fifty designs with ideas for every imaginable occasion.

Once you take the first step and decide to try your hand at dough sculpture you will need to beware – it can be addictive! You will discover that it is a very relaxing and therapeutic hobby, you must have heard of venting your anger on bread dough when kneading it to improve the quality of the dough!

No special ingredients, tools or equipment are needed, so there is nothing to deter you from 'having a go', and what could be more satisfying than producing a really professional-looking model .

As you become more experienced with using salt dough you will discover what a very versatile medium it is, in fact it is sometimes referred to as baker's clay, offering all the advantages of traditional clay without any of the hassle. I hope after scanning the pages of this book you will be inspired to try your hand at doughcraft and that you get as much enjoyment from your baking as I do.

Opposite Wind Chime Mobiles (page 74) and Father's Day Off (page 34).

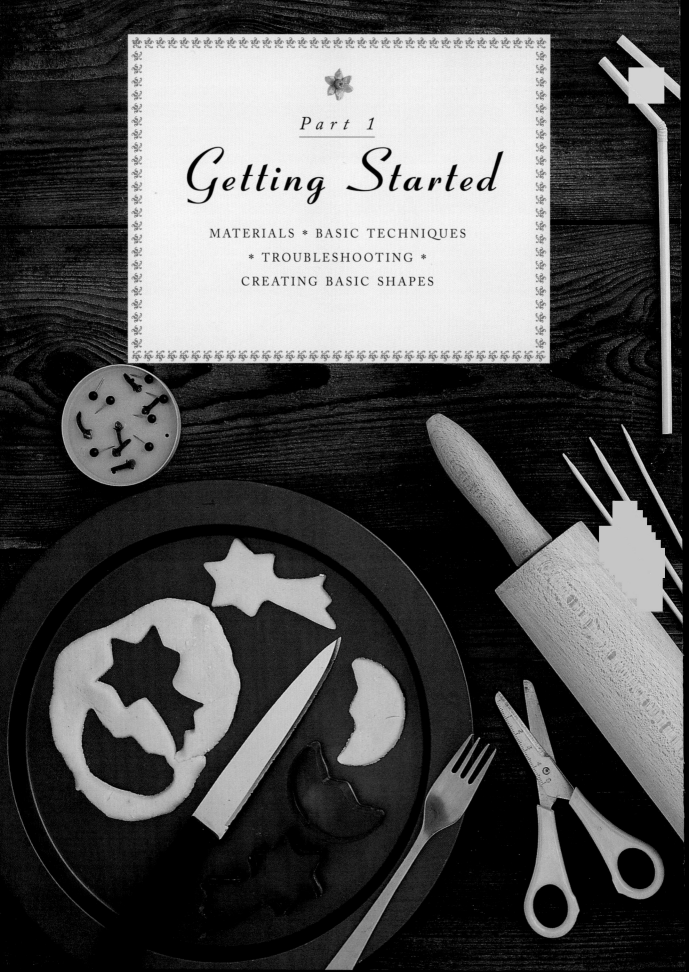

Part 1

Getting Started

MATERIALS * BASIC TECHNIQUES
* TROUBLESHOOTING *
CREATING BASIC SHAPES

✳ *Materials* ✳

THE DOUGH

The materials used to make a basic dough are flour, salt and water. There are a number of additional extras that can be added to give a slight variation, but most people will find the simpler the recipe the better.

Flour – generally this needs to be a high quality plain flour, and the higher the starch content the better the quality of the flour. Don't be tempted to buy strong flour, the sort used for conventional bread making, as it has a much higher gluten content than ordinary flour and will make the dough too elastic to model with successfully.

Salt – a fine-grain table or cooking salt is necessary for making salt dough. When the dough is first made, the grains of salt will be visible and can give a coarseness to the texture, but this will disappear after a while as the salt gradually dissolves.

Water – a smoother dough is achieved if the chill is taken off the water, helping to dissolve the grains of salt. Include a drop from a boiled kettle to your measured cold water, making sure it is only tepid or it will cause the gluten in the flour to develop.

Add the following ingredients to the basic recipe if desired:

Wallpaper paste – a tablespoon of dry paste may be added to the flour before making the dough. It contains a fungicide and so prevents mould without affecting the consistency of the dough.

Cooking oil or glycerine – a tablespoon of either may be added to the basic recipe with the water, not forgetting to reduce the amount of water to compensate for the extra liquid. They produce a slightly more malleable dough than that made with water alone, but the dough is dry to work with and you will need to use a little water to assemble your model, or you will find it falls apart when cooked. It also stays a much paler colour when baked than the basic dough, but this may be useful on occasion.

Cornflour – this is practically pure starch and does not contain any gluten, so for the purposes of doughcraft it makes a very superior dough. More water is needed if using all cornflour as it is more absorbent than wheat flour. The best results are obtained by substituting a percentage of the ordinary flour and using a mixture of the two. This gives a strong dough which can be used for extremely fine work, it is very white, hardly taking on any colour when baked, and very expensive!

PVA glue – this is the sort of water-based glue used by children in playgroups. If you substitute some of your water with this glue, adjusting the amount to compensate for the extra viscosity, you will have a stronger model, but one that is more like plastic than dough in appearance.

PAINTS

Practically any sort of paint can be used, but some are a lot easier to use than others. Avoid oil or spirit-based paints: they are expensive, require specialist mediums for thinning and mixing, and can't be wiped off if you make a mistake!

Water-based paints are the most suitable and easiest to use, and they range from the children's paintbox to expensive artists' quality water colours and acrylic paints. Powder paints are also worth considering as they are cheap, although the range of colours is very limited, but they have the advantage that they can be mixed in their powdered form with raw dough (as can cake colourings) for a totally different but not particularly attractive effect.

Water colours come in palettes, and as you need large quantities of paint to cover dough this is not an economical way of buying it. The best option is to buy water colours or gouache (poster paint) in a tube.

Acrylic paints are like a water-based version of oil paints. When used thinly they have that wonderful transparent quality that water colours have; however they are very quick drying, and their plastic-like finish acts as a protective cover on the dough, so you cannot correct mistakes unless you move quickly.

Although not actually a paint, it is worth mentioning eggwash here. An egg, whisked with a little water or milk, can be painted on the raw dough with a pastry brush before baking, or cook the dough for an hour first and then brush on the egg once the surface has hardened. It produces a wonderful golden colour and highlights the areas coated, particularly useful when making models of bread, see page 38.

✳ *Materials* ✳

VARNISH

There are many types of varnish available. Avoid specialist art and craft varnishes, including spray varnishes. They are expensive and thin in consistency, and designed for work of a much finer quality than doughcraft. A good, hard polyurethane wood varnish from a DIY shop is ideal. Don't be tempted by the new, quick-drying acrylic varnishes that are on the market, they are water-based, and will cause your paint to run, closely followed by the disintegration of your model. Non-drip varnish is the easiest to apply, and a couple of coats of this followed by a top coat of yacht varnish is the ideal combination. There is a choice of matt, silk or gloss finishes, and many of the varnishes are now coloured.

OTHER EQUIPMENT

The marvellous thing about doughcraft is that no specialist tools or equipment are required. The few basic essentials can be found in most kitchens.

1 Large mixing bowl, the bigger the better
2 Straight-sided mug
3 Sharp knife
4 Rolling pin
5 Baking sheets – salt dough will quickly damage your baking trays. The salt attacks the surface of the metal causing rusting after only a few uses. Non-stick trays are slightly more hard-wearing but will still lose their surface fairly rapidly. There is a solution to this problem; protect the trays with either tin foil or baking parchment lining. Don't use greaseproof paper, it will stick firmly to your dough. If, however, you are making large quantities of dough it would be more economical in the long run to invest in special trays. Both stove enamelled and aluminium trays are resistant to salt and will not rust. Enamelled trays are the better of the two, as aluminium becomes pitted after a time. Both these baking sheets are about four times the price of standard ones, but are worth investing in.
6 Round trays – when making garlands or any circular object it is easier to work on a round tin and follow the line of the tray to get a near perfect circle. However, round tins are not readily obtainable in either aluminium or enamel, so you will need to either line with paper, or buy a good supply of very cheap ones and discard them after a while. A pizza tray or the base of a cake tin are ideal for this.
7 Modelling tools – a never-ending selection of items can be used for modelling your dough (if you have clay modelling tools they will come in very useful). The most useful tool is a bamboo skewer used for kebabs; a cocktail stick serves the same purpose but is not as strong. Other useful items are small scissors (preferably stainless steel as chrome-plated ones will soon rust), round-bladed knife, fork, piping nozzles, large plastic straws, any small pastry or cake decorating cutters, especially flower and leaf shapes (the bowl of a teaspoon with the handle bent back out of the way makes a good leaf shape cutter). Make impressions on the dough to give an attractive, decorative effect using anything from a piece of fancy lace to buttons and bent paper-clips.
8 Brushes – several types of brush are needed for doughcraft. Firstly, you will need a soft pastry brush for applying water to join pieces of raw dough together. You will also need paintbrushes; use synthetic, artists' quality brushes, available from art and craft shops as the fibres last much longer than natural sable or bristle. Three brushes will be adequate: a No 4 round brush for fine work, a No 8 round brush for larger areas, and a 10 mm ($^{3}/_{8}$in) flat brush for stippling or large, flat areas. Finally, you need a decorator's paintbrush for varnishing – a 50mm (2in) brush is the most useful size.
9 Potato ricer or garlic press – a potato ricer is just like a giant garlic press, used in the catering industry for puréeing large quantities of potato (they are now available from good kitchen shops). Both the potato ricer and garlic press are wonderful for extruding dough to make hair, grass, sheep's wool, birds' nests, and many other things. Using the garlic press is a very labour intensive process if large amounts of extruded dough are required. It does, however, produce finer strands than a potato ricer.
10 Cloves and black-headed map pins – essential for fruit stalks and eyes and noses respectively.
11 Paper-clips – different sized paper-clips, particularly the giant ones, make ideal hangers.

✳ Basic Techniques ✳

MAKING DOUGH

The simplest way to measure out the basic ingredients for salt dough is by volume rather than by weight. The ratio of ingredients is two parts flour to one part salt and one part water. Use a straight-sided mug to measure in as a sloping-sided cup will make a difference in volume and could affect the consistency of the dough.

A good quantity of dough to start with would be:
4 mugs flour
2 mugs salt
2 mugs water

Mix the flour and salt together well in your mixing bowl and then add the water, remembering first to take the chill off the water. Do not add all the water at this stage as different brands of flour will not absorb the same amount of liquid, and the rest can be added if the dough is too dry. Once you have made a few batches you will soon be familiar with exact quantities required. Using a round-bladed knife, mix the water in well and then turn out the dough and knead thoroughly on your work surface.

Kneading is very important, as the more your dough is kneaded the smoother it will be, and the warmth of your hands helps to dissolve the grains of salt and take away the granular appearance. You should be able to tell at this stage if the consistency of the dough is right. It should be soft enough to mould readily (try rolling a ball in the palm of your hand), and yet firm enough to hold its shape. If it crumbles as you try to roll it, it is too dry so add a little water, it may be sufficient to wet your hands and re-knead the dough. If the dough sticks to your hands or to the work surface it is too wet, so you will need to add more flour. Remember, it only takes a little extra water to make it too wet, but it takes a lot of extra flour to make it dry enough again. Having kneaded the dough well for at least five minutes, leave it (no more than half an hour), covered with a plastic bag to prevent a dry skin forming.

STORING UNCOOKED DOUGH
Once your dough has been made for more than a couple of hours, the consistency will start to deteriorate, it attracts moisture from the atmosphere and becomes sticky. If you do need to leave it for a while, cover with a plastic bag as when resting, but check it before you begin again. If it feels at all sticky, it is generally less effort in the long run to make a fresh batch. Another thing that you will notice if you leave your dough for any length of time, the colour when baked is slightly darker. This means that it is not suitable to leave a model half made and finish it off at a later stage, or to use old and fresh dough in the same model.

MAKING MODELS

Specific instructions are given with each individual project, but there are a few points common to all. Firstly, check that your dough is the correct consistency. When modelling with your hands, there is no need to flour your hands as the dough will not stick to them. You will, however, need to use flour if you are rolling out with a rolling pin, exactly like rolling out pastry.

Work directly on to your baking sheet as your model will distort if you make it on a work surface and then try to move it. When assembling your dough models, dampen the relevant area slightly with a little water to join together the component parts. Too much water will produce a slippery, rather than a sticky, surface and the pieces will tend to slide around.

You will find that you need to wash your hands frequently when working with salt dough, so it helps to work near a sink. Obviously the kitchen is the ideal place as it is quite a messy pastime!

Finally, salt dough is heavy and relatively soft, and if you try to make a model that stands up, it is likely to collapse or sink down into itself. A typical example might be a snowman made by placing one ball on top of another, after a while the head will begin to sink into the body before the dough has had time to harden. A way of dealing with this problem is to use something as a frame to build your model round: this can be a scrunched-up piece of tin foil, or the cardboard middle of a toilet roll, or even a frame of shaped wire netting. The same principle applies if any part of your model needs supporting during cooking. A ball of aluminium foil placed underneath the relevant part will support it and can be removed once baking is complete.

✳ Basic Techniques ✳

USING TEMPLATES

Templates can be very useful in providing you with shapes for doughcraft designs, allowing you to achieve just the outline you want, and making it easier to repeat the shape.

Actual size templates for some of the projects in this book have been provided (see pages 118–26). To use, simply trace or photocopy the template on to thin card. Cut out the shape, lay lightly on top of the rolled-out dough and cut around the outline using a sharp knife.

The templates may also be enlarged or reduced to create larger or smaller designs. In this case, the template will need to be enlarged or reduced using a photocopier. Remember, of course, that if you do this the dough requirements will also vary with the size of the model.

MAKING A HANGER

Many pieces of doughcraft are designed to hang on the wall, and there are many suitable ways of making a hanger as follows:

1 Making a hole in the dough
Use a large plastic straw as a miniature cutter to cut a hole in your model. If you simply poke a hole with a skewer or similar, without actually removing any of the dough, the hole will close up again on baking. Once baked and varnished a piece of ribbon can be threaded through for hanging on the wall. If for any reason you forget to make a hanger, or the hole does close up during cooking, it is possible to drill through cooked dough very carefully using a small drill bit.

2 Using string or wire
A piece of string or twisted wire can be incorporated into the top of your model when you are making it. Make sure the string is strong enough as salt dough is very heavy. (The only drawback to this method is that it does not always look tidy.) If using string make a loop by knotting the ends together, then bury the knot well into the dough to anchor it, and with wire, twist the ends together and use in the same way. As the dough cooks it will swell slightly and mould itself around the string or wire holding it in place.

3 Using paper-clips
This is the most successful way of making a hanger. Simply make sure that you use the largest paper-clip possible for the size of the model and push it well down into the dough so that the end with the double loop is buried. As the dough cooks, it will rise slightly and mould itself around the loops of the clip so securing it firmly. Do not use a staple or other open-ended metal hook, as there is no way of anchoring it in the dough and it will soon come out. Hairpins are not recommended for the same reason, although the wavy spikes do provide a little security.

BAKING DOUGH

Baking doughcraft is more of a drying out process – rather like cooking meringues – and takes several hours. Dough should be baked at between 100–120°C (200–250°F/Gas Mark ¼–½), slightly lower in a fan-assisted oven. As a general rule of thumb, it needs to be cooked for one hour for every 6mm (¼in) thickness.

When cooked the dough will be golden brown and lift easily from the tray giving a hollow sound when tapped sharply on the back. If it is stuck to the tray or gives a dull sound when tapped, it is not ready and should be returned to the oven. As long as the temperature does not exceed 120°C (250°F/Gas Mark ½) the dough will not burn.

It is important that your model is thoroughly cooked and dried out right through to the centre, as any remaining moisture will either continue to dry out after cooking and cause the piece to shrink and crack or, once varnished, will be trapped and cause softening.

Every oven is different, and once you have made a few models you will soon discover the best temperature within the above range. It is also worth experimenting with moving the shelves around as different parts of the oven cook at different speed. With some of the larger models in particular, you may find it convenient to bake your dough overnight. If you are at all worried about leaving it for so long, you can always lower the oven temperature a little to compensate.

─ PAINTING DOUGH ─

*B*efore you begin to paint your dough model, ensure that it is absolutely cold. If you try to paint whilst there is still any heat in it, the paint will dry immediately and will be patchy. It may also craze, as it will if applied too thickly.

Colours can be varied according to the thickness of the paint used. For more subtle colours thin down the paint with water, whilst brighter bolder colours are achieved with thicker paint. A wide variety of colours are available straight from the tube, but if you do not wish to buy too many, any colour can be mixed from a few primary colours plus black and white. The colour wheel below will give you a guide on how to mix them. If you make a mistake when painting, simply wipe off the offending paint with a damp cloth and start again.

Some people prefer not to paint their models at all but to leave them natural. If this is the case, the appearance can be enhanced either by eggwashing the piece before you bake it as in conventional cooking, or by giving it a wash of very thin brown paint which gives a sepia effect to the finished model.

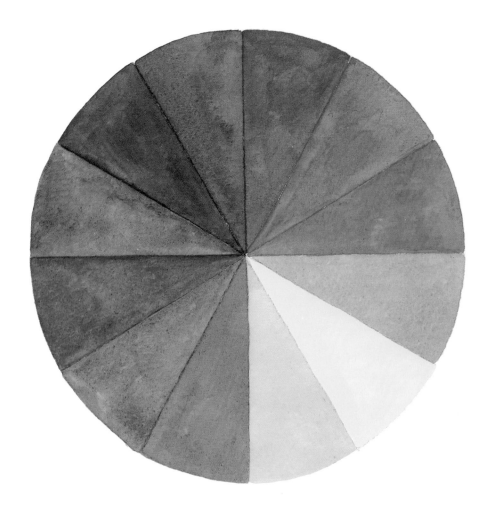

VARNISHING DOUGH

This is the most important part in the production of your model, as the varnish is necessary to protect the finished dough article. Make absolutely sure that the paint is completely dry, and indeed that the model is completely cooked right through before varnishing. Any moisture will be trapped once the varnish is applied and will cause the piece to soften and the varnish to flake. Ensure that every nook and cranny is well covered as even a pinhead-sized hole in the varnish will allow moisture through. Give your models at least two, but preferably three coats of varnish on both sides for maximum protection. It helps to wear disposable gloves to protect your hands when varnishing. The best way to apply the varnish, avoiding drips and runs, is all over in one go, leaving the varnished piece on a wire rack to dry. If you must varnish one side and then the other, place the dough on a plastic sheet to dry as the varnish will stick to paper. Beware, however, of colour or print on the plastic as the varnish may cause it to lift off and your design may be ruined.

CARE OF DOUGHCRAFT MODELS

Under normal household conditions your dough should keep for many years. If kept in an excessively damp atmosphere it may soften, but it can be re-hardened (see Troubleshooting). To clean it, simply dust or wipe with a damp cloth.

After some time you may find that a new coat of varnish will brighten a dough piece up. Do not place in steam such as near a kettle or in a steamy bathroom as this may affect the varnish. Direct sunlight should be avoided as it will fade the paint.

To store doughcraft designs, particularly the more seasonal designs such as the Christmas and Easter projects, wrap well in bubble wrap, or a similar waterproof material, and keep somewhere dry.

✻ Troubleshooting ✻

*H*aving mastered the basic techniques, you are all set to start creating your own beautiful models. If things should go wrong, don't despair – most problems are easily solved. The following is a list of the more common faults that may occur.

RISING, BLISTERING DOUGH

If the dough rises and forms bubbles during baking, this is an indication that either the dough was too wet or the oven too hot – or both! If the dough is still soft enough, pierce the bubbles with a pin and gently press back into shape. Reduce the temperature of the oven for the remainder of the cooking time. For future reference, if the dough is too soft it will not hold its shape well and detail will be lost. If the oven is too hot, the dough will start to brown slightly before it hardens. This should help you decide what caused the fault and how to avoid it next time.

CRACKS

It seems that cracks which appear during or after baking are an occupational hazard. Although they are rare, sometimes it is almost impossible to avoid them. Cracks on the reverse of your model are incidental to the baking process and are not detrimental in any way to the piece. These are the sort of breaks that you find in 'real bread'. they appear more in thicker models, and can be somewhat avoided by cooking at a lower temperature.

The cracks that are particularly upsetting are the hairline cracks that appear from nowhere after baking is complete. Changes of temperature cause slight expansion and contraction in the bread dough, causing stresses which can lead to cracking. Sometimes this happens during the cooling process, particularly with larger pieces, so it helps to cool them very slowly in the oven, gradually reducing the temperature until the oven is switched off. Leave the model in the oven until completely cool.

If cracks do appear after baking they can be filled with a little fresh dough using the same principle as a filler on plaster. If the model is already painted and varnished, leave the filler dough to dry out naturally in a warm room, and, when dry, touch up with fresh paint and varnish. It is not advisable to re-bake, as the changes in temperature may cause another crack.

SOFTENING DOUGH

If atmospheric conditions are exceptionally humid, or your dough models are kept in an excessively damp atmosphere, they may become soft and spongy. They can be re-hardened by placing them on a radiator or in the airing cupboard for several days. Alternatively, they may be placed in a cool oven (no more than 100°C (200°F/Gas Mark ¼) for 2–3 hours. This will darken the varnish slightly and will smell dreadful but will not harm your model in any way! If the varnish does show any signs of bubbling it means that the oven is too hot.

REPAIRING BREAKAGES

Salt dough is fairly durable but will break if dropped. If the break is clean and your model is not in too many pieces it can be repaired successfully with glue. Small pieces broken off can be attached with 'Superglue', but any larger pieces, or those which take any strain when the piece is hanging on the wall need something a little more substantial. A resin-based adhesive which works with a hardener, such as 'Araldite', or a very concentrated PVA craft glue such as 'Weldbond', would be suitable in this case.

If the damage is small such as an ear knocked off and lost, or the end of a leaf crumbled away, the offending part of the model can be restructured using fresh dough. With a very small repair, it is better to allow the new dough to air dry in a warm place for a few days until it is hard, rather than returning to the oven and discolouring the original varnish. When it is hard, retouch with paint and varnish.

FLAKING VARNISH

This is caused by damp or steam. The appearance of your sculpture can be improved by rubbing away the flaking varnish with a rough cloth, such as towelling, or gently with a very fine piece of emery paper, taking care not to scratch the paint underneath. Then give two coats of fresh varnish and re-hang in a drier location.

✳ *Creating Basic Shapes* ✳

ould the dough with your hands, or roll it out with a rolling pin on a lightly-floured surface, depending on the shape you are making. Shapes can be cut using pastry cutters or a sharp knife, or alternatively, if necessary, using a cardboard template made by tracing off the patterns supplied at the back of the book (see pages 118–126).

FRUIT

STRAWBERRIES
A small ball of dough, moulded to a point at one end and marked with a cocktail stick to give the effect of seeds. For the stalk use a de-seeded clove, or a small star-shaped leaf cut from a flattened ball of dough, and anchor this in place with a clove stalk

PEAR
A ball of dough elongated and narrowed at one end, with a clove stalk as in the apple, and a small leaf added.

GRAPES
Small balls of dough in a slight 'S' shape. Add leaf, stalk and vine – a spaghetti-shaped piece of dough laid on top and twisted.

APPLE
A simple ball of dough with a clove pushed in 'head-first' to make a stalk. A leaf can be added if required.

PLUMS
A small oval-shaped ball of dough, with a crease added down one side using a cocktail stick, and a hole pressed in the top. Size, shape and colour can be varied to produce cherries, peaches, apricots, etc.

ORANGE
A ball of dough 'pitted' with the blunt end of a bamboo skewer, or rolled on the zesting part of a cheese grater to give the orange peel effect. A clove with the seed broken off is used as the stalk.

BANANAS
Are best avoided!

FLOWERS

DAHLIA, MARIGOLD, CHRYSANTHEMUM

A stylised version of any of these can be made by placing a round ball of dough on top of a flattened piece and then snipping all the way round both pieces of dough with a small pair of scissors.

DAFFODIL

Assemble outer petals from flattened, elongated pieces of dough. The centre is made from a small sausage-shaped piece, flattened and then rolled up and placed on top of outer petals.

PANSY

Five petals made from flattened balls of dough, slightly pointed at one end and assembled as shown in the photograph. Push a hole in the centre with a skewer or cocktail stick.

DAISY SHAPE

This can be made from thinly rolled out dough using a small sugarcraft cutter, or moulded from a flattened ball of dough with the edges drawn up with a cocktail stick. Push a hole in the centre.

ROSE

The centre of the rose is made from a flattened ball of dough rolled up to form a tight bud. The flower is built up to the required shape by rolling successive flattened dough petals around the centre bud.

LEAVES

*L*eaves of different shapes and sizes can easily be made by moulding or cutting.

USING CUTTERS

This method is especially useful for leaves of complicated shape such as holly or ivy. Roll dough out thinly with a rolling pin and, after using the cutter, mark veins with a cocktail stick.

PINCHED LEAVES

A stylised leaf suitable for trees or hedges can be made by pinching a piece of dough between thumb and forefinger, then breaking it off. Make a number, then pile them on top of each other.

CUT LEAVES

A simple leaf can be made from a rolled out piece of dough by cutting it into long narrow strips and then cutting these into diamond shapes. Veins are marked with a cocktail stick.

MOULDED LEAVES

These can be made from a flattened ball of dough pinched to a point at one end. The sides can be drawn up with a skewer if desired to give more of an oak leaf effect. Mark veins as before.

CAULIFLOWER

As for the cabbage, but with a larger centre ball and fewer outside leaves. Pit the centre with the blunt end of a bamboo skewer, then, using the point, or a cocktail stick, divide the cauliflower head into florets.

POTATO

Roll oval-shaped balls of dough and, using the blunt end of a wooden skewer, mark three or four 'eyes' in each potato. They will look very realistic when painted.

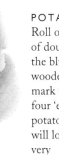

GREEN BEANS

Roll a long thin piece of dough, thinnest at the very end, and flatten roughly, making indentations with your thumb at regular intervals.

LEEK

Flatten a long sausage of dough at one end, then cut off that end in a 'V' shape. Add roots made from dough extruded through a garlic press and mark the leaves with a sharp knife. The best effect can be seen when painted.

CARROT

Roll a long pointed piece of dough, and then, using a very small circular cutter or the end of a piping tube, mark a ring in the top of the carrot. Using a sharp knife, mark fine ridges across the carrot all the way down it.

TOMATOES

Make a small ball of dough, adding a star-shaped leaf held with a clove 'stalk' as for a strawberry.

MUSHROOMS

Roll a small ball of dough, and using a very small circular cutter or the end of a piping nozzle, press about halfway into the dough to form the stalk.

ASPARAGUS

Roll a bundle of spear-shaped pieces of dough and snip the ends and shafts with nail scissors.

CABBAGE

Using a ball of dough for the centre of the cabbage, build up the outside leaves in the same way as you add the petals when making a rose.

GARLANDS

*G*arlands are a very popular subject for salt-dough models and can be formed in a variety of ways.

It is essential to keep your garlands perfectly round (assuming that you are making a circular wreath) as any misshaping will spoil the effect.

The best way to do this is to use a round baking sheet, for example a 'pizza-tray' or an upturned cake tin, of approximately the size that you wish your finished garland to be. By working directly on to this round tin and following the outline of it, you preserve the shape perfectly.

FLAT CUT-OUT GARLAND
This can be made by rolling out dough to approximately 13mm (½in) thick and then choosing two round objects of suitable size, one slightly larger than the other – for example, a saucer and a tea-plate. Place the larger plate on your dough and cut round it using a sharp knife, then, ensuring the smaller plate is central, cut round that. This will result in a hollow, perfectly circular ring which can then be used as a base for your fruit, flowers etc.

GARLANDS WITH LEAVES
Roll out a long 'snake' of dough and place it around a circular tin, about 25mm (1in) from the edge, ensuring that you leave enough space around the edge for the leaves. Press the two ends together to form a ring. Then make the leaves from flattened balls of dough following the instructions on page 17. Brush your ring with water (a paint-brush is the best tool for this), then simply place the leaves around the dough ring, pressing them lightly into position.

TWISTED GARLAND
This is made from two long rolls of dough. Before rolling your dough give it an extra knead to ensure a good smooth finish. Roll out two 'snakes' of dough approximately 19mm (¾in) thick and place them side by side. As a general guide their length should be three times the diameter of your baking tin.

With the two pieces side by side, roll them together into a twist, taking care to keep the twists even along the length of the dough.

Place the twisted length on your tin, around the edge of the circle. Join by cutting the two ends diagonally, moistening with water and pressing together.

PLAITED GARLAND
This is formed in the same way as the twisted garland but using three rolls of dough plaited together. Roll out three long snakes of dough, their length three times the diameter of your tin, and plait together, taking care to keep the shape of the plait even. A good way to prevent the plait from becoming thick at one end and thin at the other, is to start plaiting at the centre and work out towards the ends. Place on a round baking tray and join as for the twisted garland.

*T*he basic structure of any figure should be kept simple with stylised features. It is very difficult to fashion realistic-looking hands and features, so it is best not to try! Here is the basic frame to which you can add clothing or alter the stance for each individual figure.

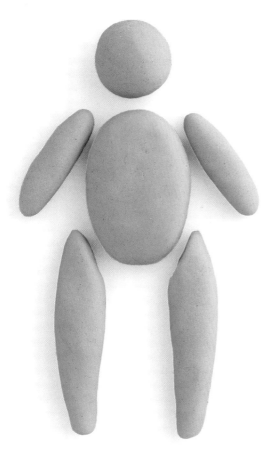

HEAD AND BODY
Create the trunk and head from two balls of dough, the larger for the body being slightly flattened.

ARMS AND LEGS
Add legs to the body and arms to the sides of the trunk. The thickness of the limbs can be varied to accommodate clothing. For a man wearing trousers, simply make the legs thicker rather than trying to add trousers on top of thin legs. The same applies to long sleeves.

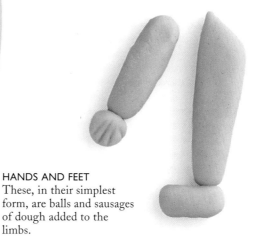

FEATURES
It is best to paint features for the most detail, although you can add a small button nose and highlight eyes and mouth by poking a hole with a bamboo skewer, to be defined with paint later.

HANDS AND FEET
These, in their simplest form, are balls and sausages of dough added to the limbs.

HAIR
By far the most satisfactory way of producing hair is to use dough extruded through a garlic press or potato ricer. Lengths of 'spaghetti' dough can be produced in this way and fashioned into any style you like.

Part 2

A Year of Celebrations

EASTER * MOTHER'S DAY

FATHER'S DAY * HARVEST/THANKSGIVING

HALLOWE'EN * CHRISTMAS

* Easter Egg Nests *

Fill these pretty nests with coloured tissue and foil-wrapped eggs to make a really attractive table decoration or an Easter gift. They can be any size from as little as 50mm (2in) up to 25cm (10in) and can be left either natural or painted brown.

To make one large or several small nests you will need:

- *2 cups of flour made into dough (page 12)*
- *Potato ricer (preferably) or garlic press*
- *Paint*
- *Varnish*

1 If making large nest roll out half the dough to 6mm (¼in) thick, and using a plate of the required size as a template for the base, cut out a circle with a sharp knife. If making small nests there is no need to use a base.

2 Using a potato ricer push sufficient dough through for the size of nest that you want to make.

4 To make the large nest place the extruded dough all round the edge of your base, piling it up quite high to stop the eggs falling out.

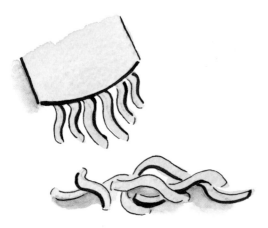

3 To make the small nests, simply gather the extruded dough together into a ball – take care not to squash it too much. Hollow out the centre of the ball with your fingers.

5 Bake, paint as desired and varnish as instructed in Basic Techniques.

✱ Easter Basket ✱

A colourful basket of spring flowers, complete with Easter bunny. You could give this basket as a gift at any time of the year by simply omitting the rabbit and varying the choice of flowers.

To make the Easter basket you will need:
- *2 cups of flour made into dough (page 12)*
- *Large paper-clip*
- *Paint*
- *Varnish*

1 Roll out half the dough to 13mm (½in) thick, and using the trace-off template on page 118 cut out a basket shape. Transfer to a baking sheet. To create a basket-weave effect use a wooden skewer to mark on the vertical lines and draw a fork horizontally across as shown. Roll two lengths of dough 6mm (¼in) in diameter and 15cm (6in) long. Twist together to make a rope, brush with a little water and lay at the base of the basket. Make a handle in the same way by using dough lengths 13mm (½in) in diameter and 45cm (18in) long.

3 Make approximately thirty small flower heads by flattening 13mm (½in) balls of dough in the hand and drawing up the edges as shown with a skewer. Push a hole in the centre of each flower. Place a cluster of flower heads in the centre of each group of leaves.

2 Make fifty rounded leaves, twenty of which should be slightly smaller. Lay the leaves on the basket as shown in five separate groups, building up the smaller leaves on top of the larger ones.

4 To make the rabbit place a small pear-shaped piece of dough for the head on top of a larger pear-shaped body as shown. Add a bobtail, long ears and a tiny ball of dough for the front foot. Mark the eyes, nose and whiskers with a skewer, and place the finished rabbit at the base of the basket.

5 Push the large paper-clip into the centre of the basket for hanging. Bake, paint as desired and varnish as instructed in Basic Techniques.

Design your own colour schemes, and once decorated, these decorative beads can be made into a necklace, ear-rings, bracelet or even a brooch.

To make this set you will need:
- *1 cup of flour made into dough (page 12)*
- *Paint*
- *Varnish*
- *Shoelace or thong for necklace*
- *Findings for brooch and ear-rings**

* Available from craft shops

1 The beads are balls of dough with a hole through the centre. It is advisable to make different size balls of dough as they look more professional if they are graduated in the finished article. Using a skewer poke a hole through the centre of each bead, re-shaping it as you do so if necessary. Make the hole a reasonable size as it is likely to close up a little on baking.

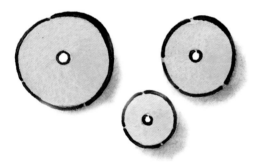

2 When the beads are made, thread them on to cocktail sticks, and support them on egg boxes to dry. (If the beads are placed directly on to the baking sheet their shape is distorted as they cook.) Allow to air dry in this way for an hour or so before baking. Make sure the beads spin freely on the cocktail sticks before putting them in the

oven, still supported on the egg boxes. This process is important as the dough is a little sticky and would weld itself firmly to the cocktail stick during baking. Check that the beads remain free during cooking.

3 To make the necklace, when the beds have been painted and varnished thread with a shoelace or thong. In between the decorated beads you could use smaller, plain coloured beads, which can be bought or made, for a more professional finish.

4 To make the ear-rings, you will need the proper findings, and again smaller beads can be used to enhance the finished ear-ring.

5 To make the brooch, roll a smooth ball of dough in your hand, and make into an oval shape, flatten to make a small plaque. Decorate around the edge with a series of holes made with a skewer or cocktail stick.

6 Bake, paint as desired and varnish as instructed in Basic Techniques.

7 Lastly, glue a brooch pin on to the back of the plaque.

This traditional flower garland incorporates the popular daffodils and violets given on Mother's Day. The plaited base provides a wide flat surface to attach the flowers to, particularly necessary for the daffodils.

To make this garland you will need:

- *3 cups of flour made into dough (page 12)*
- *Large paper-clip*
- *Paint*
- *Varnish*

1 Take two-thirds of the dough and divide it into three equal pieces. Knead each piece well and roll out into long snakes. Their lengths should be about three times the diameter of the finished garland. Plait together: if you find it difficult to keep the thickness even, try plaiting from the centre and work outwards in each direction. Make the plait into a circle following the edge of a circular baking tin, cut the ends with a knife to make a neat join.

ball of dough 25mm (1 in) in diameter, and hollowing out the centre with your forefinger. Using the tips of your finger and thumb, frill the top edge slightly. Place the trumpet of the flower over the centre join of the petals. Five of these daffodils are evenly spaced around the garland.

2 Make the daffodils by placing six pointed petals, each about 4cm (1½in) long together as shown. The trumpet centre is made by taking a

3 Place two or three small moulded leaves (see page 18) between each of the flowers, and fill in the spaces with violets. These are made by placing five small-pointed petals together, and making a hole in the centre with a skewer or cocktail stick. Finally, add a few small daisies made from flattened balls of dough with the edges drawn up as shown in Creating Basic Shapes.

4 Push a large paper-clip well into the centre top for hanging. Bake, paint as desired and varnish as instructed in Basic Techniques.

This handy key ring holder for Father's Day can be decorated in the design of your choice. Choose one of the design ideas opposite, or make up one of your own. You could personalise the gift by modelling dad's initials in dough.

To make one set of key hooks you will need:

- *1 cup of flour made into dough (page 12)*
- *3 medium-sized key hooks**
- *Paint*
- *Varnish*

* Available from hardware stores

1 Roll out the dough to 6mm (¼in) thick, and using the trace-off template on page 119, cut out the shape of the plaque. Using the trimmings, roll two long snakes of dough, each 6mm (¼in) thick and 37.5cm (15in) long and twist the two together. Dampen the outside edge of the plaque with a little water using a pastry brush and place the twisted border all round the edge, finishing off neatly in the bottom corners as shown.

2 Make the decoration of your choice, and moisten the back of it with a little water and place in the centre of the plaque. Cut a hole each side, using a plastic straw as a miniature cutter, for the plaque to be screwed to the wall.

3 Finally, gently push the key hooks into position and make sure they are all level. Do not move them about too much as the holes will be too big and they will not anchor properly. As the dough cooks, it will mould itself around the thread of the hooks, and hold them firmly in position.

4 Bake at a slightly lower temperature than usual to begin with, until the dough has set firm, to avoid the plaque rising at all. Paint as desired and varnish as instructed in Basic Techniques.

Create a model of your father relaxing with his Sunday paper. This particular model is assembled lying down, and by simply changing the style and colour of the hair, or adding a beard or moustache, you can make it very personal.

To make this figure you will need:
- *2 cups of flour made into dough (page 12)*
- *Garlic press*
- *Paint*
- *Varnish*

1 Firstly, make the rug by rolling out about a quarter of the dough to 6mm (¼in) thick, and using the trace-off template on page 119 cut out the oval rug shape. Mark all round the edge of the rug with the prongs of a fork to form the fringe as shown. The newspaper is made from a rectangle cut from thinly rolled-out dough with a crease down the centre. Place it overlapping the end of the rug.

3 Now add the arms. (In this case they are positioned before the head is attached, as the head is resting on the hands.) Make the arms thick enough to give the impression of shirt sleeves. Once the arms are in position, add balls of dough for the hands, with fingers marked as shown, and then add a ball of dough for the head, resting on the hands.

2 Make the body and legs as instructed in Creating Basic Shapes, making the legs thick enough to give the impression of jeans. Lay the body on the rug, and bend the legs up as shown. They should stay in position, but if they fall down use a piece of scrunched-up tin foil to prop them up whilst cooking. Add sausage-shaped feet, with a ridge cut in them to form the heel of the shoe.

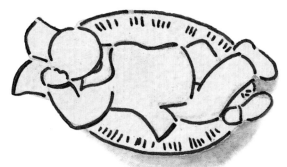

4 Place an elongated ball of dough over the top of the legs to give a 'bottom' shape. The body of the shirt is now cut from thinly rolled-out dough, cutting the tails with a sharp knife, and also cutting round the armholes to fit closely to where the arms join the body. It may be easier to drape the dough over the body and cut to shape while it is in place, being careful not to cut into the body. A small, flattened strip of dough placed round the neck makes the collar. This all looks much better once it is painted.

5 Finally, add the hair made from dough extruded through a garlic press and styled as you wish. Make a small button nose and small indented balls for ears as shown. The rest of the features are painted on after cooking, make sure the eyes are looking down at the paper when painted.

6 Bake, paint as desired and varnish as instructed in Basic Techniques.

* Harvest-time Bowls *

These attractive dishes overflowing with harvest-time goodies make a very colourful table decoration. Bake the dough directly in the terracotta dishes and varnish when the painting is finished

To make one large dish or a selection of small ones you will need:

- *3 cups of flour made into dough (page 12)*
- *Aluminium foil*
- *Terracotta plant pot saucers*
- *Cloves*
- *Paint*
- *Varnish*

1 The model would be too heavy if the whole thing was filled with dough, the pot is, therefore, filled with a base of crumpled aluminium foil on to which the fruit or vegetables are built up. The foil must be well crushed down otherwise the dough will collapse it and the fruit will sink down into the bowl. The dish should be filled with crushed foil, level to the rim.

2 Make an assortment of fruit following the instructions in Creating Basic Shapes and place on top of the tin foil. The pineapple is made from an oval ball of dough marked diagonally in both directions with the back of a knife, and a de-seeded clove stuck in each resulting square. Long, thin, flat leaves are added at the top. Make sure that none of the foil shows through in the dish by filling any spaces with small currants, grapes, plums or strawberries, and a few strategically placed strawberry flowers.

3 For the bowl of vegetables, follow the instructions in Creating Basic Shapes.

4 When the arrangement of fruit or vegetables is complete, bake the whole thing in the oven. This will not damage the terracotta bowl. Paint as desired and varnish as instructed in Basic Techniques.

Bread Basket and Cheese Board

*I*deal at a Thanksgiving dinner, this basket and fruit-adorned cheeseboard look really attractive. The bread is baked directly in the basket and left unvarnished for a more natural look, but this does make it more susceptible to the damp. The fruit is attached to the cheeseboard by magnets, to allow for washing and to stop it moving when in use.

To make the basket and board you will need:

- *3 cups of flour made into dough (page 12)*
- *4 strong, flat magnets (see page 82)*
- *Poppy and/or sesame seeds*
- *Bread basket*
- *Cheeseboard*
- *Paint*
- *Varnish*

BREAD BASKET

1 Make an assortment of bread rolls as follows. Plaits are made by plaiting together three snakes of dough which taper at each end. Cottage loaves are made by placing a small ball of dough on top of a larger one, marking lines round the edge of both with a knife, and poking a hole through the centre with a skewer. Knots are made by tying a single knot in a sausage of dough tapered at each end. Bloomers or farmhouse rolls have their tops scored with a knife. Different finishes can be given to these rolls by brushing with water and sprinkling with poppy or sesame seeds, dusting with flour or brushing with eggwash.

2 Arrange the rolls in the corner of the basket, and add a few ears of wheat made by snipping a small cigar-shaped roll of dough with scissors as shown. Fill in any spaces with pea-sized balls of dough with a clove pushed into each centre.

3 Finish off the basket with a little mouse made from a cone of dough with a thinly rolled tail. The mouse's ears are small balls of dough flattened and folded, and attached with a little water. The eyes are pushed in with a cocktail stick. Using a little water, stick the mouse on to the basket. Bake as instructed in Basic Techniques.

CHEESEBOARD

4 The fruit for the cheeseboard is assembled on a base of leaves; instructions can be found in Creating Basic Shapes. Place two magnets sticky side down on a baking tray, wet them thoroughly and assemble fruit and leaves on top.

5 Bake, paint as desired, and varnish the fruit as instructed in Basic Techniques. Using a strong glue, attach two magnets to the cheeseboard, making sure that they line up with those on the dough model and that the polarity is right so that they attract rather than repel each other.

✳ Hallowe'en Jack o' Lantern ✳

This unique pumpkin is cleverly backed with yellow tissue paper so that when hung in front of a window, or other light source, you get the effect of a candle glowing inside.

To make the Jack o' Lantern you will need:
- *2 cups of flour made into dough (page 12)*
- *Large paper-clip for hanging*
- *Yellow tissue paper*
- *Paint*
- *Varnish*

1 Make the dough into a large ball, and then using a rolling pin flatten it to approximately 19mm (³⁄₄in) thick. The circle does not have to be completely round. Make a slight indentation in the top as shown ready for the stalk, and using the back of a knife mark vertical curved lines.

2 Cut out the eyes, nose and mouth with a sharp knife.

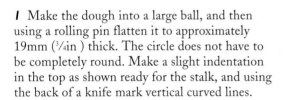

3 Use the trimmings to make a stalk and attach this to the top of your pumpkin.

4 Push a large paper-clip into the top for hanging. Bake, paint as desired and varnish according to the instructions in Basic Techniques.

5 When the varnish is completely dry, glue a circle of yellow tissue paper on to the back of the pumpkin.

Winnie Witch

This rather trendy witch with her moons and stars outfit is great fun for Hallowe'en. The figure seems complicated at first glance, but taken step by step she is quite straightforward.

To make the witch you will need:
- *Length of wooden doweling or other suitable stick*
- *Bundle of twigs*
- *Strong, brown rubber band*
- *2 cups of flour made into dough (page 12)*
- *Garlic press or potato ricer*
- *Large paper-clip*
- *Paint*
- *Varnish*

1 Attach twigs to the end of the wooden stick with the strong rubber band. The finished broomstick should be about 30cm (12in) long.

2 Make the figure as instructed in Creating Basic Shapes, but varying the position as described here. Place the body of the witch above the broomstick as shown. Add a leg on top of the broomstick, and the other, from the knee down only, as though it were coming from behind the broomstick. Place head in position.

4 Make pointed feet at the bottom of the legs, using rolls of dough for the boot cuffs. Make hair from extruded dough, add a pointed nose and tall hat. Mark eyes and mouth with a skewer, and add finer details when painting.

3 Roll out a sheet of dough for the dress, cut a triangular piece and lay this over the body and broomstick. Make the arms with a long sausage of dough, cover in a triangular sheet of dough for the sleeve, position so that the witch is holding the broomstick. Mark the hand with a skewer. Use a sheet of dough for the cape, make a stand-up collar from a flattened sausage.

5 Make the cat from two balls of dough. Add sausage legs, pointed ears and a long tail. For the face add two small flattened balls of dough, and a small ball for the nose. Mark on whiskers, eyes and claws, and perch on the handle.

6 Push a large paper-clip into the hat for hanging. Bake, paint as desired and varnish as instructed in Basic Techniques.

✳ *Christmas Tree Decorations* ✳

These colourful Christmas tree decorations can be decorated with paints, glitter, sequins, lace, etc. The traditional Father Christmas decoration is slightly more complicated as it is individually constructed but well worth the effort.

To make a selection of tree decorations you will need:

- *2 cups of flour made into dough (page 12)*
- *Paper-clips*
- *Sequins of different sizes*
- *Glitter*
- *Ribbon for hanging*
- *Paint*
- *Varnish*

1 To make the mini garland, twist together two snakes of dough, each 6mm (¼in) thick, and bend round into a circle approximately 50mm(2in) in diameter. Make a couple of leaves and a few berries to place over the join.

2 The bells and the candles can either be made from rolled-out dough so that the decorations are flat, or they can be moulded by hand to give a three-dimensional effect. Finish off with leaves and berries.

3 For the Christmas tree, roll out the dough to approximately 6mm (¼in) thick, and cut out a tree shape. To make the pot, mould a piece of dough in your hand to a pot shape, then lay over the trunk of the tree. Cut the edges and base with a knife to neaten the shape, then lay a flattened snake of dough across the top to form the rim of the pot. Add a dough bow to decorate the front of the pot.

4 The poinsettia is constructed by laying six pointed petals, with a line marked down the centre of each, on top of four leaves. Small balls of dough make the stamens.

5 The figures for the Father Christmas and angel are made as instructed in Creating Basic Shapes, but on a much smaller scale, each being approximately 10cm (4in) high. Add a hat, fur trim, beard and belt to the Santa figure, and place a sack in his hand. For the angel, a pair of wings tucked under her back, long flowing hair, and a triangular-shaped dress with a rounded collar complete the figure.

6 Make sure that all your decorations have a hole (cut using a plastic straw) or paper-clip hook for hanging on the tree, and bake as instructed in Basic Techniques. Paint your decorations on both sides, as they will be seen from all sides when hanging on the tree. Varnish as instructed, and finish the decoration by gluing on glitter or sequins for the angel's halo and the decoration on her dress as well as the balls on the tree.

These beautiful table decorations will brighten up any table, particularly when lit. It is, however, safer to use coloured night-lights as a tall candle would need a manufactured wooden or metal candlestick as a base.

To make one candle ring you will need:

- *2 cups of flour made into dough (page 12)*
- *Holly leaf cutter or template (page 120)*
- *Night-light*
- *Paint*
- *Varnish*

1 Take half the dough and divide it into two equal pieces. Roll each piece into a long snake, approximately 25mm (1in) in diameter and 30cm (12in) long, and twist the two snakes of dough together into a rope. Remove the candle from its metal case, and make a ring with the dough rope around the case. Cut the ends with a sharp knife and join neatly with a little water. If you bake the candle holder with the dough, it will be held firmly in place. When the dough has finished baking slip the candle back into the holder. When the candle is used up, simply replace it with a fresh one.

3 To make the ring decorated with poinsettias, follow the instructions for the flowers on page 44, making them smaller to fit on to the candle ring. You could, however, vary the theme by using ivy leaves or Christmas roses.

4 Bake, paint as desired and varnish according to the instructions in Basic Techniques

2 To make the decoration for the ring, roll out the rest of the dough and using either a holly leaf cutter or the trace-off template on page 120, cut out several holly leaves. Mark the veins with a skewer and position the leaves around the edge of the ring as shown. From the trimmings, make berries from pea-sized balls of dough and add between the leaves.

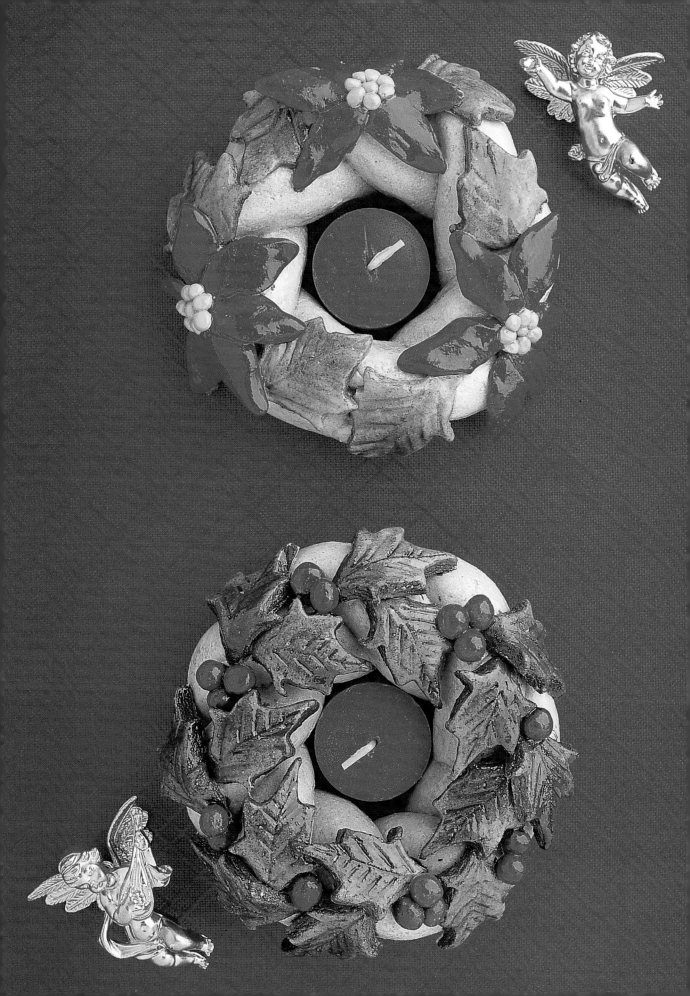

* Golden Christmas Swag *

This beautiful swag, given an antique gold effect finish, will add a touch of sophistication to your festive decorations.

To make this garland you will need:
- *3 cups of flour made into dough (page 12)*
- *Holly leaf cutter or template (page 120)*
- *Giant paper-clip*
- *Aerosol can of matt black resin lacquer**
- *Metallic gold wax finish for plaster castings**

* Available from art and craft shops.

1 Divide the dough into four even-sized pieces. Roll three pieces into long ropes 60cm (24in) long and 25mm (1in) in diameter. Plait together, starting from the centre and working out in each direction to ensure an even result. Loop the plait around into a tear-drop shape and transfer to a baking sheet. Trim the ends neatly.

2 Roll out the remaining piece of dough to 6mm (¼in) thick. Using either a holly leaf cutter or the trace-off template on page 120, cut out twenty-one holly leaves. Mark the veins with a wooden skewer. Position leaves in groups of three evenly around the plait, brushing first with a little water. Place three berries made from pea-sized balls of dough in the middle of each group. Press a hole in each berry with a wooden skewer.

3 To make the bow, mould two large triangles from the dough trimmings. Place these, pointed ends touching, at the top of the swag. Use a skewer to mark on the creases. For the ribbons, roll two sausages of dough and flatten them with the palm of your hand. Trim the ends to an inverted V-shape with a sharp knife and place on the garland as shown. A small flattened ball of dough makes the bow's knot and hides the joins.

4 Push the giant paper-clip into the top of the swag for hanging. Bake according to instructions in Basic Techniques.

5 Working in a well-ventilated area, spray one side black. When dry, turn over and spray the other. The resin lacquer has a waterproof finish so serves the same purpose as a varnish, but ensure the surface is covered entirely. Leave to dry.

6 Rub gold wax into the surface of the dough using a soft cloth as directed on the pack. Alternatively the process can be speeded up and less wax used if it is applied with a wide, flat, stiff-bristled paintbrush. Keep the gold to the surface of the dough, so that the black still shows in the recesses. Polish the painted swag by buffing with a soft cloth until it shines.

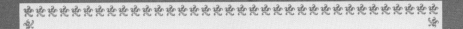

Part 3

Tokens of Love

VALENTINE'S DAY * ENGAGEMENT

WEDDING * ANNIVERSARY

Make a small dough heart for your loved one. They can be personalised by painting names and dates if you wish, or you may choose to add lace or flowers as shown.

To make a selection of hearts you will need:

- *1 cup of flour made into dough (page 12)*
- *Heart-shaped cutter or cardboard template (page 120)*
- *Lace and dried or silk flowers*
- *Glue*
- *Ribbon*
- *Paint*
- *Varnish*

1 Roll out the dough to approximately 6mm (¼in) thick, and cut out heart shapes using a sharp knife. You may use a heart-shaped cutter if you have one, or if you prefer, use the trace-off template on page 120 which can be reduced or enlarged as required. Or you could cut the heart shapes freehand. These may not turn out symmetrical, but they can be very charming.

3 For the twisted heart, roll out two snakes of dough approximately 6mm (¼in) in diameter and 30cm (12 in) long. Twist these together into a rope. Cut into two 15cm (6in) lengths and use for the two sides of the heart, joining at centre top and bottom neatly as shown. The birds are made from small pieces of dough as shown, and the wings and tails are snipped with scissors.

4 Before baking the hearts, cut a hole with a plastic straw for threading through a ribbon for hanging.

5 Bake, paint as desired and varnish according to the instructions in Basic Techniques.

2 Decorate the hearts as required. For the different flowers, follow the instructions in Creating Basic Shapes, or you can glue silk or dried flowers on to your model after baking and varnishing. Similarly, the lace is glued into place after baking and varnishing.

NOTE The hearts at the bottom of the photograph are made in clay cookie moulds which are readily available in a wide variety of designs. They should come complete with instructions, but basically the mould is lightly oiled and floured and then the dough is pressed into the mould and the edges trimmed. Turn the mould over and tap out the dough which should be impressed with the design. Cut a hole with a plastic straw for a hanging ribbon, before baking.

✳ *Valentine's Garland* ✳

*T*his pretty garland with red ribbons and roses would make a lovely Valentine's gift. It is obviously more complicated than the previous project, but if you are experienced in doughcraft you will not find it too difficult.

To make this garland you will need:
- *3 cups of flour made into dough (page 12)*
- *Large paper-clip*
- *Paint*
- *Varnish*

1 To make the basic garland, roll out a snake of dough approximately 25mm (1in) in diameter and 60cm (24in) long. Place this around the outside edge of a round baking tin, such as a pizza tray or upturned cake tin, to give you a circle of approximately 20cm (8in) diameter, ensuring that you leave enough space around the edge for the leaves. Make twelve leaves from a flattened a 25mm (1in) diameter ball of dough, following the instructions for moulded leaves in Creating Basic Shapes. Place these leaves all around the edge of the garland as shown, attaching with a little water if necessary.

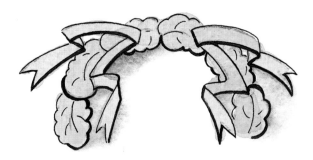

3 Make several moulded leaves as instructed in Creating Basic Shapes, and place them at the centre top of the garland covering the ends of the ribbons as shown.

2 Make the ribbons by rolling out four snakes of dough 15cm (6in) long and 13mm (½in) in diameter. Flatten these by pressing along the length with the palm of your hand, and trim one end into an inverted V-shape. Place on the garland as shown.

4 Make several roses, both full blown and rose buds, as instructed in Creating Basic Shapes, and place in a cluster at the top of the garland, overlapping the leaves.

5 Push a large paper-clip into the top for hanging. Bake, paint as desired and varnish according to the instructions in Basic Techniques.

✳ *Love-bird Candle Holder* ✳

Celebrate an engagement with this special gift. The love-birds are exquisitely modelled around a commercially manufactured candlestick and the result is a very professional-looking gift.

To make this candlestick you will need:
- *1 cup of flour made into dough (page 12)*
- *A metal or wooden 'Wee Willie Winkie' type candlestick*
- *Paint*
- *Varnish*

1 Make several moulded leaves as instructed in Creating Basic Shapes. Brush the candlestick with a little water and place the leaves around the base as shown.

2 To make five small flowers, join together five petals at their points and place a tiny ball of dough over the join. Place these in a ring around the centre.

3 Make the two love-birds from small pieces of dough as shown, snipping their wings and tail with scissors and marking the eyes with a skewer or cocktail stick. Place them facing each other and leaning against the centre of the candlestick.

4 Bake on the candlestick, paint as desired and varnish according to the instructions in Basic Techniques.

This pretty wall plaque design is based on the lovers' knot, and would make a most fitting gift for an engagement. It is usually a complicated knot to tie, but when made from salt dough we cheat, and by making it in two dimensions the process is simplified.

To make the wall plaque you will need:
- *2 cups of flour made into dough (page 12)*
- *Large paper-clip*
- *Paint*
- *Varnish*

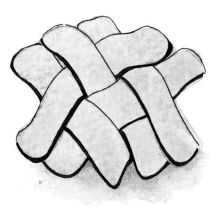

1 Roll out five sausages of dough approximately 19mm (¾in) in diameter and 12.5cm (5in) long, and flatten them by pressing with the palm of your hand. Weave these five strips together diagonally as shown; you will then begin to see the knot taking shape.

2 When the strips have been woven you will see a triangular space at each end of the knot. Make two balls of dough 25mm (1in) in diameter, flatten them and tuck underneath the woven strips to finish off the knot. Having completed the knot, mark each strip with the prongs of a fork to give a rope effect.

3 Make small, moulded leaves, roses and violets as instructed in Creating Basic Shapes. Place pairs of leaves all around the edge of the plaque, and the flowers at the centre of each pair of leaves, alternating between violets and roses.

4 Make a bow from a flattened snake of dough folded over and trimmed to an inverted V-shape at each end. Wind another strip of dough around the centre of the bow. Place the finished bow in the centre of the plaque and add a large paper-clip at the centre top for hanging.

5 Bake, paint as desired and varnish as instructed in Basic Techniques.

* *Wedding Spoons* *

These traditional bride's favours make the ideal gift to be given to the bride by the bridesmaids and the page-boys. Place spoons face down on a baking tray after soaking in water for a few minutes. Position dough directly on to the spoons' backs.

To make the wedding spoons you will need:

- *Wooden spoons of varying sizes*
- *1 cup of flour made into dough (page 12)*
- *Paint*
- *Varnish*
- *White ribbons*

——— BELL SPOON ———

3 Make five small leaves and place points together, in the centre of the horseshoe. Place a small flower, made by flattening a ball of dough in the hand and drawing up the sides with a cocktail stick, over the centre join. Push a hole in the middle of the flower head.

1 To make the bells take two small balls of dough approximately 25mm (1in) in diameter and mould into shape. Hollow out the underneath of the bells with your thumb, and place a tiny ball of dough in the centre of each hollow to make the clapper. Add a bow made from flattened strips of dough as shown.

——— ROSE SPOON ———

——— HORSESHOE SPOON ———

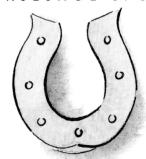

4 Roll out a sausage of dough 6mm (¼in) in diameter and 20cm (8in) long. Flatten then trim the ends to an inverted V-shape with a sharp knife. Twist the dough to give the effect of a bow and streamers. Place three small leaves and a rose (see page 18) over the centre.

2 Roll out a dough sausage 13mm (½in) in diameter and 10cm (4in) long. Flatten and bend into a horseshoe shape. Trim the ends. Pinch up a little of the dough at the centre bottom edge and use a skewer to make nail holes all round.

5 Bake the decorated spoons, paint as desired and varnish as instructed in Basic Techniques. Tie long white ribbons around the handles for carrying.

These charming and amusing figures would make a very original wedding gift particularly if the pair are designed to look like the real bride and groom! The basic structure is kept simple and it is quite easy to match hair colour and styles.

To make the bridal couple you will need:

- *3 cups of flour made into dough (page 12)*
- *Garlic press*
- *2 paper-clips*
- *Paint*
- *Varnish*

1 Make the bodies as instructed in Creating Basic Shapes, and place side by side on the baking tray. Begin by positioning the groom's body, head and legs, making the legs wide enough to look like trousers. Now make the bride in the same way, adding a pair of voluptuous boobs!

2 The groom's collar, tie and jacket are added next, cut from thinly rolled-out dough. It may be easier to drape the rolled-out dough over the body and cut to shape in place, taking care not to cut into any other parts.

3 The bride wears a two-tier skirt, made from triangular pieces cut from thinly rolled-out dough. Cut across the top of the triangles at the waist, and ensure that the skirt touches the groom's trouser leg so that the two figures are attached together. Add the bride's right arm, lying down by her side ready to hold the flowers. Next, add the frill across her neck and shoulder, and another at the bottom of each tier of the dress.

4 Add the interlinked arms as shown. Make the groom's left arm, rolled thick enough to give the impression of his jacket sleeve. His feet are two sausages of dough attached to the bottom of his trousers.

5 The hair is made by pressing some dough through a garlic press, and styled any way you choose. Any other desired features such as eyes, mouth, ears and noses are added next. You may wish to paint on some of the features after baking.

6 The final touch is the groom's top hat and bride's bouquet, as well as the flowers in her hair

and his buttonhole. These little flowers and leaves are made as instructed in Creating Basic Shapes.

7 Push a paper-clip for hanging into the top of each of their heads. Bake, paint as desired and varnish according to the instructions in Basic Techniques.

These individual picture frames, painted with either an antique gold or antique silver effect, would make an ideal anniversary gift – particularly for a special one such as a gold or silver wedding anniversary.

To make an anniversary photo frame you will need:

- *Plain wooden photograph frame of appropriate size for photograph*
- *1 cup of flour made into dough (page 12)*
- *Aerosol can of matt black resin lacquer**
- *Metallic gold or silver wax finish for plaster castings**

* Available from craft shops.

1 This decoration is actually assembled on the frame, and the whole thing is then baked in the oven. Remove the backing and glass from the frame so that you are left with only the wooden surround. It is preferable to have an unfinished wooden frame as the dough will adhere better to the wood, and the flatter the surface of the frame the better (in this case you will probably find that the cheapest wooden frame you can find is the best). If this is not possible, the decoration can easily be glued into place after baking.

2 Wet the frame where the decoration is to go and begin to add the dough pieces. Two different designs are shown: a more modern design for the silver wedding, and a traditional one for the golden wedding. The modern design is a series of small hearts cut from thinly rolled-out dough and spaced around the edge of the frame between small leaves and daisy-type flowers, made as instructed in Creating Basic Shapes.

3 Make the roses and leaves for the traditional design as instructed in Creating Basic Shapes and arrange across opposite corners of the frame. Begin by placing the leaves on the edge of the frame, and then add a selection of roses of different sizes on top of the leaves. Place the largest rose in the centre and work outwards with the smaller ones.

4 Bake the frame as instructed in Basic Techniques. You will find that it will not take long to cook, probably only an hour or two.

5 To paint the frame, spray with matt black resin lacquer all over. This is quick drying, and the metallic wax can be added about half an hour later. The wax is best applied with a wide, flat, stiff-bristled paintbrush rather than a cloth. Keep the gold or silver to the surface of the dough so that the black shows in the recesses.

6 Do not varnish as the black lacquer is waterproof, and you will destroy the metallic effect if you apply varnish. Simply buff up with a soft cloth to shine, and reassemble your photograph in the frame.

This pretty garland of roses and forget-me-nots would make a lovely gift for a special anniversary or wedding. To personalise the gift, you could add a banner of dough across the garland with a date or initials.

To make a heart-shaped garland you will need:
- *3 cups of flour made into dough (page 12)*
- *Large paper-clip*
- *Paint*
- *Varnish*

3 Make several more leaves and a selection of roses of different sizes as instructed in Creating Basic Shapes. Place the leaves and roses around the top of the heart as shown in the photograph. Begin with the largest rose in the centre and work outwards in each direction, making sure the flowers are evenly spaced.

4 When the roses are in place, add a few smaller leaves between them. Finally, make a lot of little forget-me-nots by flattening a very small ball of dough and drawing up the edges with a stick as instructed in Creating Basic Shapes. Place these in clusters in the gaps between the roses.

1 Take four pieces of dough and roll each into a snake, approximately 19mm (³⁄₄in) thick and 37.5cm (15in) long. Twist them together in pairs to make two ropes. Place these ropes on your baking sheet to make the two halves of a heart shape as shown. Trim neatly at centre top and bottom, and join with a little water.

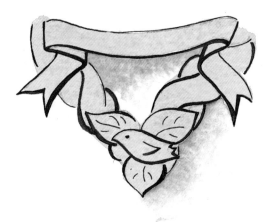

5 Place a piece of scrunched-up tin foil in the centre of your garland to act as a support for the banner. To make the banner, roll a snake of dough approximately 19mm (³⁄₄in) wide and 20cm (8in) long and flatten it with the palm of your hand; trim the ends to look like a ribbon. Lay the banner over the piece of scrunched-up tin foil in the centre of the garland, folding over at the ends as shown.

2 Make three moulded leaves as instructed in Creating Basic Shapes, and place these at the bottom of the heart as shown. Sit a small love-bird on top of the leaves, made in exactly the same way as the birds on page 56.

6 Bake, paint as desired and varnish as instructed in Basic Techniques.

Part 4

Birthdays for Everyone

YOUNG CHILD * TEENAGER

COMING OF AGE

MOTHER * FATHER * GRANDPARENTS

ALEX

A decorated name plate for a child's bedroom door or an initial would be a lovely personal birthday gift for a small child. This basic design can be adapted for children of all ages.

To make several name plates or initials you will need:

- *1 cup of flour made into dough (page 12)*
- *Paper-clips*
- *Sticky pads*
- *Paint*
- *Varnish*

1 To make the flat plaque for a door, roll out a piece of dough to 6mm (¼in) thick and cut out the basic shape. Add your decoration on to this plaque, and leave enough room to paint in the required name.

2 There are two ways these plaques can be made to fix to the door. If they are fairly small and light, they can be attached with a couple of sticky pads. If they are larger, or somewhat heavier, it is best to cut small holes each side with a plastic straw, and then the finished plate can be screwed to the door.

3 To make an initial with a teddy bear, roll out a snake of dough approximately 19mm (¾ in) thick and make your letter from this about 12.5cm (5in) high. Letters such as 'C' or 'S' can be made with one continuous piece, but for a letter which will need joins, such as 'E', you use a little water to join all the parts and make sure all parts are firmly attached.

4 To make the teddy bear follow the instructions on page 72, but remember to reduce the size to a height of 50mm (2in). The difficulty comes in placing the teddy on the initial. The teddy will affect the centre of gravity of the finished piece, and you must take this into account when positioning the teddy on to the initial. Do make sure that the final model is well-balanced as shown.

decorated with doughcraft such as flowers or animals, or the decoration can be painted. When making a name, it is important to make sure that the letters are joined together in as many places as possible for strength. Wet the letters as you join them and make sure they are firmly attached. If in doubt about the durability, add a base by placing a flattened sausage of dough along the bottom of the letters. If it is difficult to push a paper-clip into a name without distorting it, simply hook the actual name over a couple of pins stuck in the wall, alternatively you can fix them to wall or door with a couple of sticky pads.

5 Complete names are simply an extension of the single initial. The entire name can be

6 Bake, paint as desired and varnish according to the instructions in Basic Techniques.

✻ Rag Doll and Teddy Bear ✻

These traditional characters would be much appreciated by young children The rag doll could be personalised to have the same hairstyle as its recipient, and perhaps the same dress, whilst the teddy's bow tie could be made to co-ordinate with the child's bedroom.

To make one of each of these figures you will need:

- *2 cups of flour made into dough (page 12)*
- *Black-headed map pins for teddy's eyes and nose*
- *Garlic press or potato ricer*
- *Paper-clips*
- *Paint*
- *Varnish*

--------- T E D D Y   B E A R ---------

1 Roll an oval ball of dough approximately 75mm (3in) tall for the body. Use a golf ball sized ball of dough for the head. Roll sausages for the arms and legs, mark the pads and paws with the end of a plain piping nozzle.

2 Place a ball of dough on the face for the muzzle, and use a skewer or cocktail stick to mark the mouth. Add black-headed map pins for the eyes and nose. Make the bow tie from two long triangular dough pieces joined at the point, with ribbons cut from thinly rolled-out dough. Place a small ball of dough over the join to neaten.

--------- R A G   D O L L ---------

3 The body, head and legs are made as instructed in Creating Basic Shapes. Add a simple dress made from two layers of thinly rolled-out dough cut into shape; the collar is made from two small flattened sausages of dough. Now add the arms, roll wide to give the impression of sleeves as shown. Little balls of dough are added at the end of the sleeves for hands.

4 A very small button nose is added, and eyes and mouth are marked with a cocktail stick. The hair is made from dough extruded through a garlic press or potato ricer and styled as desired. The shoes and socks are painted on after baking.

5 Push paper-clips into the top of the models and bake. Paint as desired and varnish according to the instructions in Basic Techniques.

✳ *Wind Chime Mobiles* ✳

The ever-popular wind chime mobiles make ideal gifts for children of any age, particularly teenagers. The basic design can be adapted to suit any style but remember to paint your pieces both sides as they will be seen from all directions as they move in the breeze.

To make one set you will need:
- *2 cups of flour made into dough (page 12)*
- *Thread*
- *Paint*
- *Varnish*

3 Bake, paint as desired and varnish according to the instructions in Basic Techniques.

4 When the pieces are finished, cut five pieces of thread of different lengths, and use these to join each one of the smaller pieces to the large central model.

1 When you have decided on which design to make, use the trace-off templates on page 121. Roll out the dough approximately 6mm (¼in) thick, and using a sharp knife cut out the required shapes as shown.

2 Use a plastic straw to cut five holes along the bottom edge of the large piece and one hole in the top. Cut one hole in the top of each of the five smaller pieces.

5 Finally, loop a length of thread through the hole in the top of the large piece for hanging.

These comical figures cannot fail to amuse even the most difficult-to-please teenager. The basic structure of the dolls is kept simple with exaggerated features.

To make a teenage figure you will need:
- *2 cups of flour made into dough (page 12)*
- *Garlic press*
- *Split rings for ear-rings if required**
- *Paper-clip*
- *Paint*
- *Varnish*

* Available from hardware shops

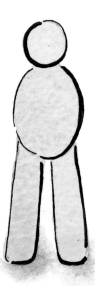

1 Make the basic figure as instructed in Creating Basic Shapes, making the legs wide enough to give the impression of trousers if required.

3 Hair is made from dough extruded through a garlic press and styled as desired. A small button nose can be added, and eyes and mouth are marked with a skewer and defined with paint later. If making a figure with short hair, don't forget to add some ears!

4 Push a paper-clip into the top of the head for hanging. Bake, paint as desired and varnish according to the instructions in Basic Techniques.

2 Add the clothing as desired. Clothes are made from thinly rolled-out dough cut to shape with a sharp knife. It may be easier to add any shirts or jackets before positioning the arms.

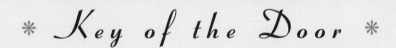
These keys are designed to celebrate the all-important coming of age (either eighteen or twenty-one). There is a traditional mortice key or a modern Yale type key for the more up-to-date.

To make a key you will need:
- *1 cup of flour made into dough (page 12)*
- *Gold or silver paint*
- *Varnish*

— MORTICE KEY —

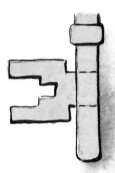

1 Cut out the teeth of the key first from a flattened piece of dough using a sharp knife. Leave a long piece on the straight side to attach to the stem of the key as shown. Roll a snake of dough approximately 13mm (½in) thick and 15 cm (6in) long for the stem, and lay on top of the teeth as shown. Wind a small, flattened sausage of dough around the stem just above the teeth.

2 Roll an oval-shaped ball of dough for the handle of the key, and flatten it with the palm of your hand. With a sharp knife cut out the centre as shown. Add some personal details (name, age, date, etc) to the handle of the key by 'engraving' with the point of a skewer.

3 Attach the handle to the stem. The join will have to be reinforced or it will break, to do this insert a piece of wooden cocktail stick across the join as shown.

— YALE KEY —

4 Roll out the dough to 6mm (¼in) thick and make a circular impression on the dough with the top of a glass or a round cutter. To make the handle of the key, cut around the outside of the mark, 2mm (¹⁄₁₆in) from the impression, and stopping short of completing the circle, cut the stem of the key with a straight edge on one side, and a jagged-toothed edge on the other side.

5 Cut a hole in the top with a plastic straw, and make a groove down the length of the key with a sharp knife. Personalise the key by adding details where the number of the key would normally appear.

6 Bake, paint gold or silver and varnish as instructed in Basic Techniques.

Another way to celebrate coming of age, or any other birthday, is to give an individual gift of the relevant numbers personalised for the recipient. Construct the basic number and choose your own design.

To make a decorated number you will need:

- *1 cup of flour made into dough (page 12)*
- *Garlic press*
- *Paper-clip for hanging*
- *Paint*
- *Varnish*

1 Roll the dough into snakes 19mm (³⁄₄in) wide and make up numbers as required. If you have difficulty getting the numbers to look right, try drawing them on a piece of baking parchment and laying the dough on top. Remember to wet any joins for extra security.

2 Add a platform to the bottom of the number to hold it together safely, then begin the decoration of your choice.

3 To make a figure that appears to hang from the 8 simply place a head and hands looking through the top, and a skirt and legs in the bottom part of the number. Hair is made from dough extruded through a garlic press and the other features are painted on after baking.

4 Alternatively you could take a decoration from another project in this book. The beer mug from page 32 has been chosen to decorate our number 21. To personalise the decorated number, add a name at the bottom as shown. You could also add a date if you wish.

5 Push a paper-clip into the top for hanging, making sure that you judge the centre of gravity correctly so that the number hangs straight. Bake, paint as desired and varnish according to the instructions in Basic Techniques.

❋ Fridge Magnets ❋

All these designs have been kept simple so that even a child could make them for a parent's birthday. Almost any small design can be made into a fridge magnet but ensure that the magnet is strong enough as the dough shapes can be quite heavy.

To make a selection of magnets you will need:
- *1 cup of flour made into dough (page 12)*
- *Magnets*
- *Paint*
- *Varnish*

1 Firstly, place the magnets on the baking tray 'sticky' side down, this is the side which sticks to the fridge door. (There is usually a small spot on the side of the magnet that will not stick; so make sure that you have this facing upwards.) Wet the magnets and place your decoration on top.

2 Flowers and fruit make excellent subjects for fridge magnets, and detailed instructions for making both can be found in Creating Basic Shapes. Vegetables and bread rolls are also perfect, and for the more ambitious small animals or even figures always look good. To make a cat follow the instructions on page 96.

3 To make a pig, roll out a snake of dough 6mm (¼in) wide and 10cm (4in) long. Cut into two equal lengths and fold each in half as shown for the legs.

4 For the pig's body, place a flattened ball of dough over the legs, and another smaller one for the head. The nose is a very small ball of dough, and the ears are small, flattened sausages. Eyes and nostrils are marked with a skewer.

5 Bake the magnets, and when cooked you will find that the dough is firmly welded on to the magnet. This is a much more permanent way of joining the two rather than gluing after varnishing. Paint as desired and varnish according to the instructions in Basic Techniques.

✳ *Birthday Flower Vase* ✳

These beautifully decorated vases are very simple to make, and as the dough is made up around jam jars they even hold water for fresh flowers. They can be used for a variety of purposes and make holders for dried flowers, kitchen utensils or even toothbrushes!

To make a decorated vase you will need:
- *2 cups of flour made into dough (page 12)*
- *Clean jam jars (interesting shapes are best)*
- *Paint*
- *Varnish*

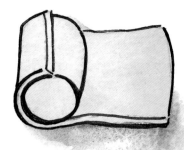

1 Measure the height and circumference of the jam jar at its widest point. Roll out the dough to 6mm (¼in) thick, and with a sharp knife cut a rectangle the size of the measurements taken. Wet the jar and lay it on its side on top of the dough. Carefully roll the dough around the outside of the jar joining the two cut edges together neatly.

3 Add the decoration of your choice to the vase, making sure that it is firmly attached with a little water. Do not make it too large or heavy as it may move out of position during baking. Detailed instructions for making flowers are given in Creating Basic Shapes.

4 Stand the vase upright on the tray and bake in the oven. Paint as desired and varnish according to the instructions in Basic Techniques.

2 Stand the jar upright, and carefully mould the dough to the shape of the jar in the places where the jar narrows. Trim the top and/or bottom with a flattened snake of dough or a rope made from two snakes twisted together.

Pencil Pot and Paperweight

These would make ideal presents for a father's birthday and have therefore been kept simple so that children can make them.

To make pencil pot and paperweight you will need:
- 2 cups of flour made into dough (page 12)
- Cardboard toilet roll tube
- Paint
- Varnish

1 Measure the height and circumference of the toilet roll tube. Roll out half the dough to 6mm (¼in) thick, and with a sharp knife cut a rectangle to fit the tube according to your measurements. Brush the outside of the tube with a little water. Lay it on its side on top of the dough and roll around the tube, joining the cut edges neatly. Roll out another small circle of dough, and stand the tube on it and trim to size to make the base of the pot. Transfer to the baking tray.

2 Roll four snakes of dough 6mm (¼in) thick and about 25cm (10in) long, and twist them together in pairs to make ropes to trim the top and bottom edges of the pencil holder. The rows of circles making the patterns round the holder are impressed with a plastic drinking straw.

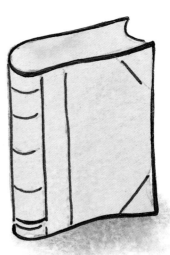

3 To make the paperweight, roll out the dough to 25mm (1in) thick, trying to keep at least one straight edge as you roll. Use the straight edge for the spine of the book and cut the other three sides with a sharp knife to give you a rectangle approximately 12.5 x 8cm (5 x 3½in). Using the side of your finger, try to indent the three cut sides so that the edges of the book are slightly concave rather than flat. Mark lines along all three edges to give the effect of pages. Lastly, using the blunt edge of the back of a knife, mark the spine and corners of the book as shown.

4 Bake, paint as desired and varnish according to the instructions in Basic Techniques. Don't forget to paint and varnish the inside of the toilet roll.

This smart roadster is every father's dream. It would look particularly effective on a specially cut panel of wood, but if not mount it on a slice of log which is readily available from florist's shops.

To make the vintage car plaque you will need:
- 1 cup of flour made into dough (page 12)
- Wooden base
- Paint
- Varnish
- Picture eyes and cord

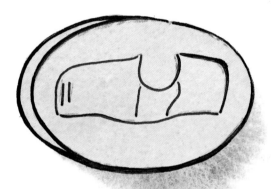

1 Roll out the dough to 25mm (1in) thick, and using the trace-off template on page 120 cut out the basic shape of the car. Wet the wooden plaque and position the car body on it. Mark the door and radiator grille with a sharp knife.

3 The bumpers at front and rear are small flattened sausages of dough with little over-riders added. The running board is a flattened snake of dough placed along the bottom edge of the car, shaped around the wheels. Model the rest of the trim, the headlamp, windscreen, steering wheel, spoiler, seat, door handle and bonnet motif from small pieces of dough and position on the car.

4 Bake, paint as desired and varnish according to the instructions in Basic Techniques.

5 When your model is dry, screw picture eyes into each side at the back, and thread a cord through for hanging.

2 Next add the wheels – these are slightly flattened balls of dough; mark the hub caps with the end of a piping nozzle and the spokes with a sharp knife. Place the wheels overlapping the car body, and support each wheel with a small ball of dough underneath so that they don't fall off. These will not be visible when the plaque is hanging on the wall.

✳ Daisy Photo Frame ✳

These pretty daisy frames are an ideal way to frame pictures of the children for their grandparents. They are simple enough for a child to make and make a perfect birthday gift.

To make the daisy photo frame you will need:
- *1 cup of flour made into dough (page 12)*

- *Picture frame without glass*
- *Piece of mount card to fit frame.*
- *Photographs showing children's faces no more than 25mm (1in) across*
- *Sticky pads*
- *Glue*
- *Paint*
- *Varnish*

1 Make the required number of flower heads (one for each grandchild) by joining a number of pointed petals at the centre, overlapping each other slightly as shown.

2 Make the daisy stalk with as many stems as you have made flower heads, and add pointed leaves to the sides of the stems.

3 On a baking sheet transfer the flower heads into position at the tops of the stems. Make sure that the flowers will fit within the frame. Cut a circle out of the centre of each flower head using a small circular cutter, or cut around a coin or other suitable round object with a sharp knife.

4 Bake, paint as desired and varnish according to the instructions in Basic Techniques.

5 When the daisy is finished, cut the photographs to size and glue behind each flower head, the eldest child behind the tallest flower, and so on down to the smallest. Stick the flower on to the mount card using several sticky pads, taking care that they don't show. Finally, mount the finished article into the frame.

These homely characters make the perfect gift for all grandparents, particularly those new to the role! The basic structure of the figures is kept simple with stylised features. This gives them a comical appearance, and ensures that they will be given and received in good part.

To make both figures you will need:

- *3 cups of flour made into dough (page 12)*
- *Garlic press*
- *2 paper-clips*
- *Small metal split rings for glasses**
- *Wire cutters*
- *Strong glue*
- *Paint*
- *Varnish*

*Available from hardware shops.

1 Make two basic bodies 20cm (8in) high (see Creating Basic Shapes). For Grandad mould the legs much wider to give the impression of trousers.

2 Before adding the arms, dress the figures. Use a sharp knife to cut out Grandad's sweater and

Granny's dress from dough rolled out to a thickness of 6mm (¹⁄₄in), and place in position over the bodies. Now add the arms. To make Granny's shawl cut two triangles from the rolled-out dough and lay over her shoulders. Mould the ties from small pieces of dough, placing a small ball over the join for the knot. Add the collar and brooch at the neck of the dress. Use a skewer to add decorative details to the clothes.

3 Now add the facial features to bring the characters to life. The hair is made by pressing some dough through a garlic press and can be styled any way you choose. Add a small ball of dough for the nose and mark on the nostrils, eyes and mouth with a wooden skewer. Make each pair of spectacles from two tiny split rings joined across the bridge of the nose with a half split ring cut with the wire cutters. The spectacles will not adhere to the dough during baking, but it is a good idea to bake your figure with them in place to ensure that they sit well on the face. Glue them in place after baking.

4 Push a paper-clip into the top of the heads for hanging. Bake, paint as desired and varnish as instructed in Basic Techniques.

Part 5

Congratulations

GOOD LUCK * BIRTH OF A CHILD

GRADUATION/EXAM SUCCESS

NEW HOME * RETIREMENT * BON VOYAGE

✳ *Good Luck Wishes* ✳

Send a 'Good Luck' message in the form of a black cat or horseshoe, either on its own or to decorate a card.

To make a 'Good Luck' card you will need:

- *1 cup of flour made into dough (page 12)*
- *Card with opening in the front**
- *Sticky pads*
- *Paint*
- *Varnish*

* Available from craft and embroidery shops

——— BLACK CAT ———

1 Place a small ball of dough for the head, on top of a larger one for the body, making sure that the cat will fit into the card opening. Small, pointed ears are added on top of the head, and a curly tail running up the cat's back. The cat is finished off with a pretty bow at its neck, made from two small triangles of dough with pointed ends touching, and ribbons cut from thinly rolled-out dough. A small ball of dough at the centre hides the join.

——— HORSESHOE ———

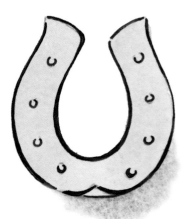

2 The horseshoe is made in exactly the same way as instructed on page 60. Make sure that the size of the horseshoe will fit into the card opening. You may prefer to decorate it with flowers as on the wedding spoons (page 60), or paint in a style that is reminiscent of barge painting as shown in the photograph.

3 If you prefer not to mount your piece on to a card but hang it on the wall, push paper-clips into the top for hanging before baking. Bake, paint as desired and varnish according to the instructions in Basic Techniques.

4 When the model is dry attach it to the card with several sticky pads, making sure that they don't show. If the card is a little flimsy for the weight of the dough, reinforce the back by sticking it on to a piece of thicker card. You may also like to add the words 'GOOD LUCK' on the front of the card.

✳ Baby's Potty ✳

The birth of a baby deserves special congratulations and these 'potties' are extremely quick and easy to make, and the decoration can be as simple or intricate as you wish.

To make a 'potty' you will need:

- *1 cup of flour made into dough (page 12)*
- *Paper-clips*
- *Paint*
- *Varnish*

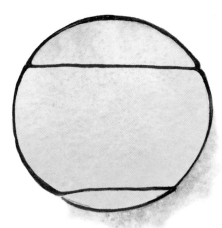

1 Break off a small amount of dough and reserve for the handle and trim of the potty. Use as much of the remaining dough as needed to make the potty the required size. Knead it very well, and roll into a large ball. Flatten the ball slightly with the palm of your hand, and using a sharp knife trim the top and bottom in a straight line as shown.

2 Trim the top and/or bottom edges of the pot with snakes of dough, using either two snakes twisted together for a pretty effect, or a single strip for a plainer version. Roll out a snake of dough about 13mm (½in) in diameter and 10cm (4in) long for the handle. Flatten this with the palm of your hand and attach to the side of the pot with a little water as shown.

3 Push a paper-clip into each side at the top of the pot for hanging, and bake, paint as desired and varnish as instructed in Basic Techniques.

✳ *Cradle with Rainbow* ✳

This is slightly more complicated than the previous project and requires some understanding of the laws of perspective! The rainbow over the baby's head symbolises hope and eternity, and the colours can be changed to co-ordinate with baby's room.

To make the cradle you will need:

2 cups of flour made into dough (page 12)

2 paper-clips

Paint

Varnish

1 Roll out the dough to 6mm (¼in) thick, and using templates on page 122, cut out the base, ends and sides of the cradle. Add the headboard to the base and mark it with a heart.

2 Add a sausage-shaped body and small round head for the baby with a little worm of dough for a topknot. Cover the baby's body with the quilt, made from thinly rolled-out dough marked with

the back of a knife. (Mark the squares on the quilt at an angle so that the perspective looks right.) Finish with a lacy trim made from very thin dough cut with a sharp knife and patterned with the point of a skewer.

3 Add the sides first then the foot of the cradle, so that the edges of the quilt are covered, giving the impression of being 'tucked in'. Decorate the foot of the bed in the same way as the headboard. Add three small balls of dough for the feet of the cradle. You may find that the right-hand side of the bed needs supporting, and this can be done by placing a roll of scrunched-up tin foil behind it during baking.

4 Finally add the rainbow over the head of the cradle. Add two paper-clips for hanging as it will not hang straight on the wall with just one.

5 Bake, paint and varnish as instructed in Basic Techniques.

✳ *Graduation Scroll* ✳

The skill in this project lies in decorating the scroll with all the personal details which mean so much to the recipient. This design can be adapted to congratulate somebody for passing any sort of exam, or even a driving test by simply altering the wording on the scroll.

To make a scroll you will need:

- *1 cup of flour made into dough (page 12)*
- *2 paper-clips*
- *10cm (4in) red ribbon 6mm (¹⁄₄in) wide*
- *Small coin*
- *Paint*
- *Varnish*

1 Roll out the dough to approximately 6mm (¹⁄₄in) thick, and using the trace-off template on page 123 cut out the scroll shape with a sharp knife. Brush the top and bottom edges with water, and roll over the two edges and stick down to the main body of the scroll as shown.

2 From the trimmings roll a ball of dough approximately 19mm (³⁄₄in) in diameter and place on the scroll near the bottom right-hand corner. Press a small coin or round, engraved object into the dough to give the impression of a seal.

3 Push two paper-clips into the top for hanging, and bake as instructed.

4 When painting give the outside edges a wash of thin brown paint to give the effect of ageing. Paint the seal red and add the wording of your choice. It is a good idea to practise the lettering on a piece of paper first, but as long as you are using water colours, any mistakes can be wiped off.

5 Varnish according to the instructions in Basic Techniques. When dry, glue the piece of ribbon, cut into two equal lengths with the ends neatly trimmed, on to the scroll touching the seal.

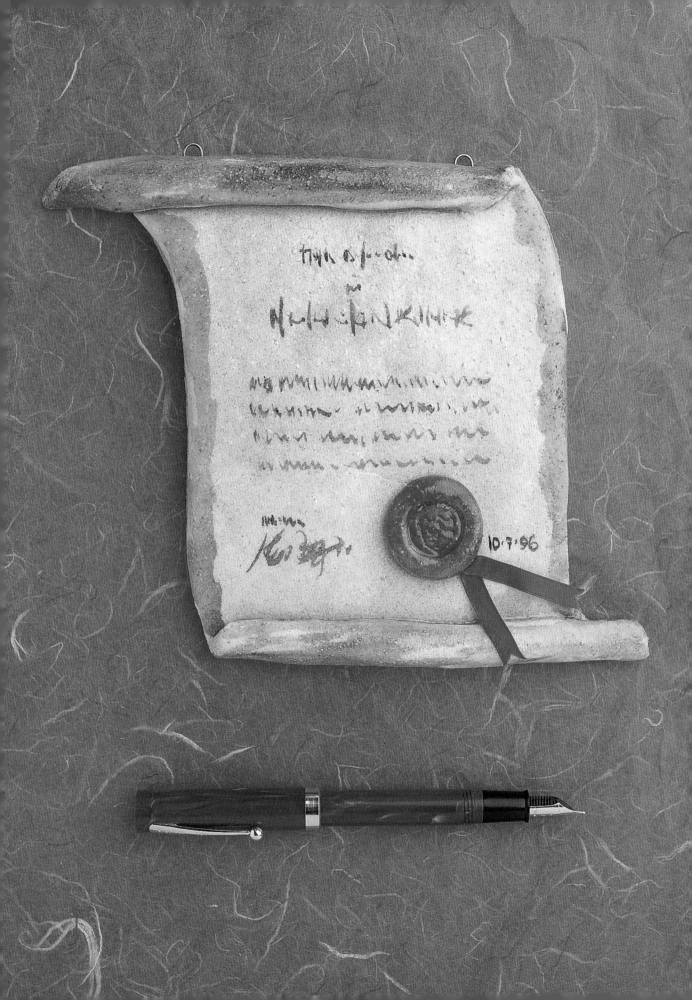

❋ The Graduate ❋

This unique and fun figure would make the perfect gift for a new graduate. The basic structure is kept simple, and like all the other figures in the book the features can be changed to match those of the recipient.

To make the figure you will need;

- *2 cups of flour made into dough (page 12)*
- *Garlic press*
- *Paper-clip*
- *Paint*
- *Varnish*

2 The mortarboard is constructed in two parts, after adding the hair. A triangle of very thinly rolled dough is placed on the head, with the point coming down towards the centre of the forehead. A rectangle of slightly thicker dough is then placed on top as shown. The tassel is made from dough extruded through a garlic press. Add a small ball of dough for the nose and mark on the eyes and mouth with a wooden skewer.

3 Add a paper-clip for hanging. Bake, paint and varnish as instructed in Basic Techniques.

1 Make the figure as instructed in Creating Basic Shapes. If making a male figure, make the legs thick enough to give the impression of trousers, or for a female figure add a skirt cut from rolled-out dough, a belt can be added at the waist. The gown, complete with wide sleeves, is cut from thinly rolled-out dough, folded back along the front edges, and the straps at the neck are two elongated triangles cut from very thin dough.

German folklore tells that salt dough brings prosperity to the home by virtue of the fact that it contains the necessary ingredients for sustaining life. This simple design can be personalised by adding the number or name of the new home.

To make the front door plaque you will need:

- *2 cups of flour made into dough (page 12)*
- *Ribbon*
- *Paint*
- *Varnish*

1 Take half of the dough and roll to about 6mm (¼in) thick, cut a rectangle for the door 12.5 x 20cm (5 x 8in). Mark the four panels with a knife and then highlight with thin strips of dough attached on top of the knife marks. The surround to the door is made from strips of dough 13mm (½in) wide, mitred at the top corners.

2 Add a doorstep cut from rolled-out dough, and on this place a doormat which is made from a flattened dough sausage with the ends fringed with a knife or the prongs of a fork.

3 Either side of the door, bay trees are made by placing a flattened ball of dough on top of a rolled trunk, and then covering with tiny leaves, made according to the instructions in Creating Basic Shapes. The barrels are moulded by hand and the planks marked with a knife.

4 Finally, the letterbox and knocker are added, with a small ball of dough for the door knob.

5 Using a plastic straw, cut a hole in the top of the door frame for hanging, then bake, paint as desired and varnish according to the instructions in Basic Techniques. You may wish to personalise this project and this is easily done by adding a name or message such as 'Welcome' to the doormat, and a number on the door.

This 'Gingerbread House' style cottage is a lovely decoration for any kitchen, and as with the previous gift of salt dough is the most appropriate gift for somebody moving into a new home.

To make the cottage you will need:
- *2 cups of flour made into dough (page 12)*
- *Garlic press*
- *Paper-clip*
- *Paint*
- *Varnish*

1 Roll out the dough to 6mm (¼in) thick, and using the trace-off template on page 124, cut out the cottage shape with a sharp knife.

3 Mark the front door, windows and bricks on the chimney with a sharp knife. Outline the door and windows with thin snakes of dough, slightly flattened. Place a small ball of dough on the door for the handle. See illustration below left.

2 Using the trimmings, roll to 3mm (⅛in) thick, and using a small round cutter, or a coin as a template, cut out a number of 'chocolate drop' style tiles for the roof. Wet the roof area of the cottage, and position the tiles in overlapping rows.

4 Cut four shutters from rolled-out dough and position either side of the windows, marking the wood effect with a knife. Mark the heart shapes with the point of a stick and cut the diamond shapes with a knife. A strip of dough is placed at the base of the door for the step. Finally, the cottage is finished off by the addition of grass along the base, made from dough extruded through a garlic press.

5 Push a paper-clip into the top for hanging. Bake, paint as desired and varnish according to the instructions in Basic Techniques.

✳ *Taking It Easy Chairs* ✳

These armchairs, complete with knitting or pipe and slippers, are a fun yet appropriate gift for somebody reaching retirement age. The armchairs can be made to either hang on the wall or be freestanding, as you prefer.

To make an armchair you will need:
- *2 cups of flour made into dough (page 12)*
- *Cocktail sticks*
- *Paper-clip*
- *Paint*
- *Varnish*

1 To make the more feminine chair, begin with the back. Roll a ball of dough in the hand until it is smooth, and then flatten with the palm of your hand to a thickness of about 25mm (1in). Try to retain the correct shape for the top of the chairback. Trim the bottom edge straight with a sharp knife.

2 The base and seat are added next, made from thick slabs of dough moulded into shape with the hands. Although they give the impression of standing out a long way from the back of the chair, this is in fact of an optical illusion, and they are not much thicker than the back. Add a frill made from thinly rolled-out dough around the base of the chair, and finish it off with a long, very thin snake of dough to look like piping.

3 The arms of the chair are short, fat sausages with a circle marked in the front end with a piping nozzle. Roll a small ball of dough and mark it with a knife to look like wool. Place very small balls of dough on the end of two cocktail

sticks to make needles, and push these through the ball of wool and put it on the chair. Push a paper-clip into the top for hanging.

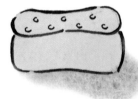

4 The masculine Chesterfield has a base and seat made from two slabs of dough moulded with the hands, and placed one on top of the other. The seat is 'buttoned' by pushing a pencil point into the dough at regular intervals.

5 The back and arms are made in one piece, from a piece of dough 19mm (³⁄₄in) thick, cut to size and buttoned. Wrap this around the back and sides as shown. Mark the shape of the front of the arms with a skewer.

6 The pipe is made from a piece of cocktail stick with a small hollowed-out ball of dough for the bowl. The slippers are made by cutting the soles from thinly rolled-out dough. Cut the tops to the shape shown, and bend over to join the soles. Place these touching the chair. Finally, the magazine is a folded rectangle of thinly rolled-out dough.

7 As these chairs are particularly solid objects, they will require slower baking than usual to avoid any cracking. Place in the oven at 100°C (200°F/Gas Mark ¼) for several hours until the model feels solid to the touch. It will still not be cooked right through, but as long as the outside feels hard it is safe to turn up the oven to the usual heat, so that the model can cook through to the centre. It may take as long as thirty-six hours to cook completely.

8 Paint as desired and varnish according to the instructions in Basic Techniques.

This wonderful herbaceous border would be a source of inspiration to any gardener. This design is ideal for the active gardener coming up for retirement, and does not contain any particularly difficult techniques.

To make the garden scene you will need:

- *2 cups of flour made into dough (page 12)*
- *Garlic press*
- *Paper-clip*
- *Paint*
- *Varnish*

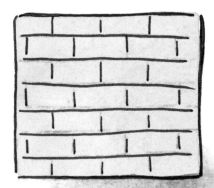

1 Take half the dough and roll out to approximately 13mm (½in) thick. Cut out a rectangle 17.5 x 15cm (7 x 6in) for the wall, and using a knife mark in the brick pattern.

3 Finish off the scene by adding a strip of grass along the base, made from dough extruded through a garlic press.

4 Push a paper-clip into the top of the plaque for hanging. Bake, paint (you can paint in some extra leaves and/or flowers on the wall to vary the effect), and varnish according to the instructions in Basic Techniques.

2 Now build up the flowers, beginning with the roses climbing up the wall and work your way down to the low plants at the front. Instructions for making a variety of flowers can be found in Creating Basic Shapes. Remember to add some leaves in between the flowers for the foliage.

✴ Bon Voyage ✴

This splendid ship is a super way to say 'Bon Voyage' to anybody embarking on a sea journey. The three-dimensional effect is achieved by building up the model in layers, and the majority of the detail is added with paint.

To make the ship you will need:
- *2 cups of flour made into dough (page 12)*
- *2 paper-clips*
- *Paint*
- *Varnish*

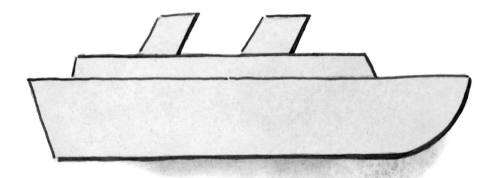

1 Take half the dough and roll to 6mm (¼in) thick, and using the trace-off template on page 125, cut out the complete ship shape. Roll the rest of the dough, and this time cut out a second ship without the funnels. Brush the first ship with water, and lay the second ship on top. Cut out the third layer, which is the hull of the ship only, and add in the same way.

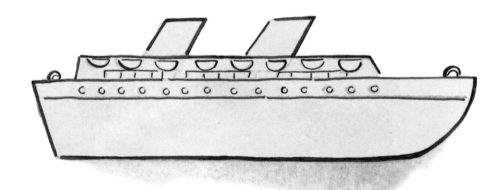

2 Mark a line across the top of the hull and using a plastic drinking straw mark portholes all the way along this section. With a knife, mark windows in the upper deck, and add a row of little banana-shaped lifeboats all the way along the top edge.

3 Push a paper-clip into each end of the ship for hanging. Bake, paint as desired, adding as much or as little detail as you wish, and varnish according to the instructions in Basic Techniques.

This wonderful hot air balloon, decorated in your own individual style, is another way of wishing luck to anybody going away.

To make a hot air balloon you will need:

- *2 cups of flour made into dough (page 12)*
- *Garlic press*
- *Thread*
- *Ribbon*
- *Paint*
- *Varnish*

1 Roll out half the dough to 6mm (¼in) thick, and using the trace-off template on page 126, cut out the balloon shape with a sharp knife. With the back of a knife, mark the vertical seams as shown. Using the plastic straw, cut a hole in the top of the balloon for hanging, and another in each corner at the bottom for attaching the basket.

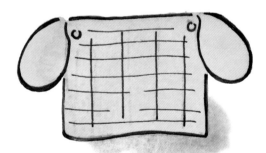

2 To make the basket, cut a square from rolled-out dough, and mark the weave effect with a skewer. Cut holes with the straw in both the top corners for attaching to the balloon. Add chunky sandbags hanging from each side of the basket.

3 The figures are made from the waist up only. Follow the instructions in Creating Basic Shapes, and give the gentleman a baseball cap, and the lady a roll-neck sweater. Hair is made from dough extruded through a garlic press, and features marked with a cocktail stick.

4 Bake, paint as desired and varnish according to the instructions in Basic Techniques.

5 When dry, attach the balloon to the basket with lengths of thread tied through the holes, ensuring that they are both the same length so that the basket does not hang unevenly. Tie ribbon through the hole in the top of the balloon for hanging.

✳ *Templates* ✳

These templates are for specific projects and are actual-size. To use, simply trace or photocopy the template on to thin card. Cut out the shape, lay lightly on top of the rolled out dough and cut around the outline using a sharp knife.

The templates may also be used to enlarge or reduce designs. In this case the template will need to be enlarged or reduced using a photocopier. Remember, of course, that dough requirements will also vary with the size of the model.

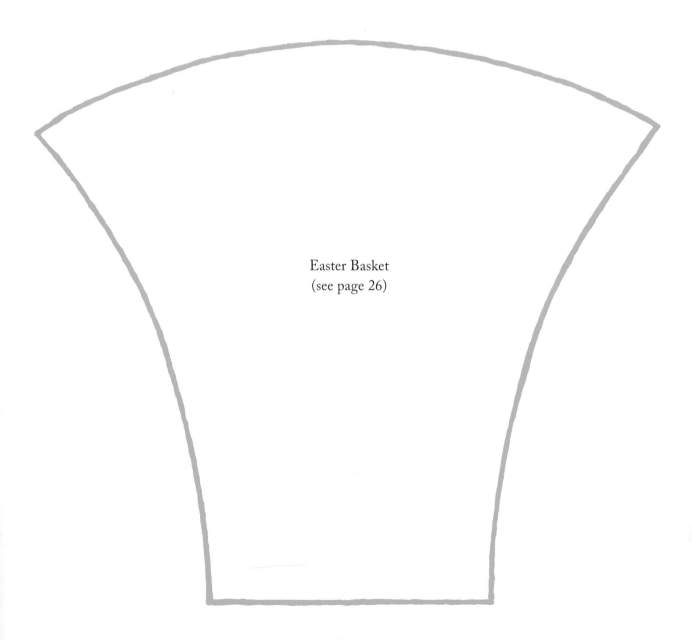

Easter Basket
(see page 26)

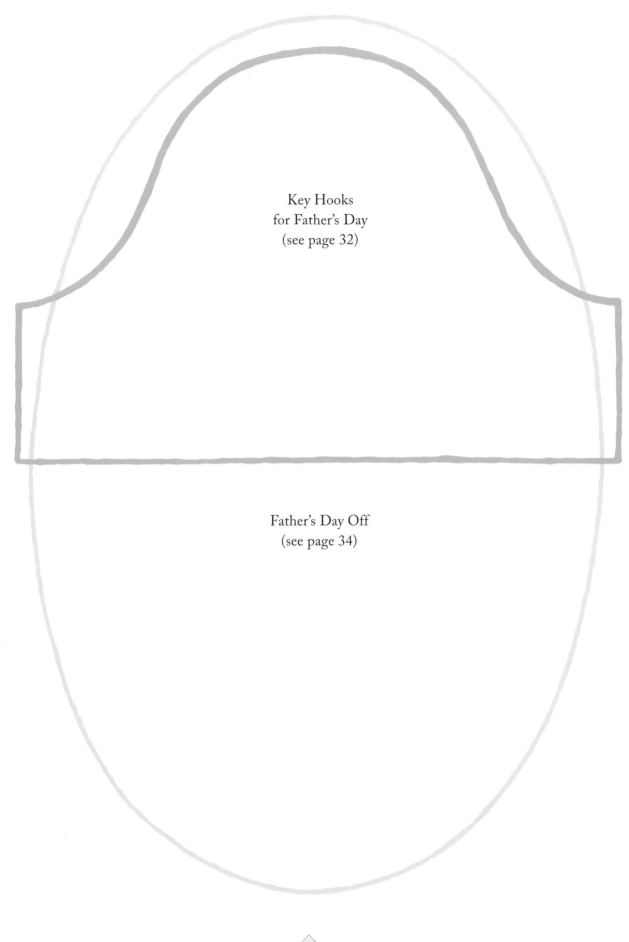

Key Hooks
for Father's Day
(see page 32)

Father's Day Off
(see page 34)

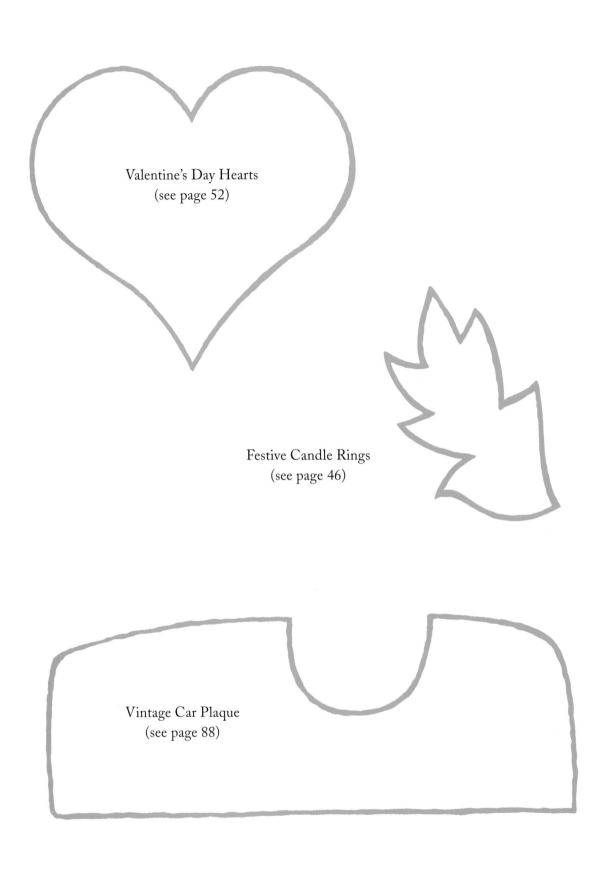

Valentine's Day Hearts
(see page 52)

Festive Candle Rings
(see page 46)

Vintage Car Plaque
(see page 88)

Wind Chime Mobiles
(see page 74)

Cradle with Rainbow
(see page 100)

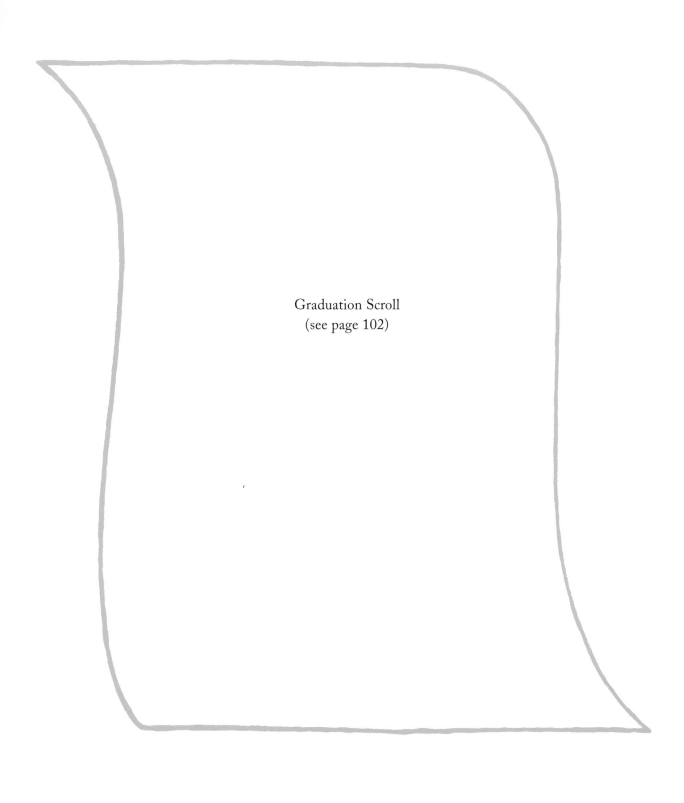

Graduation Scroll
(see page 102)

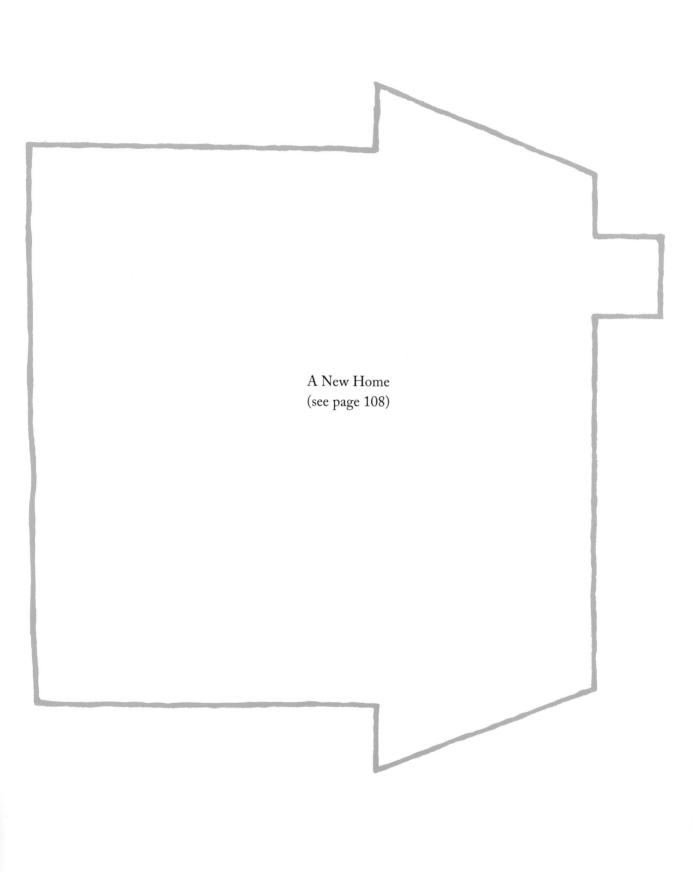

A New Home
(see page 108)

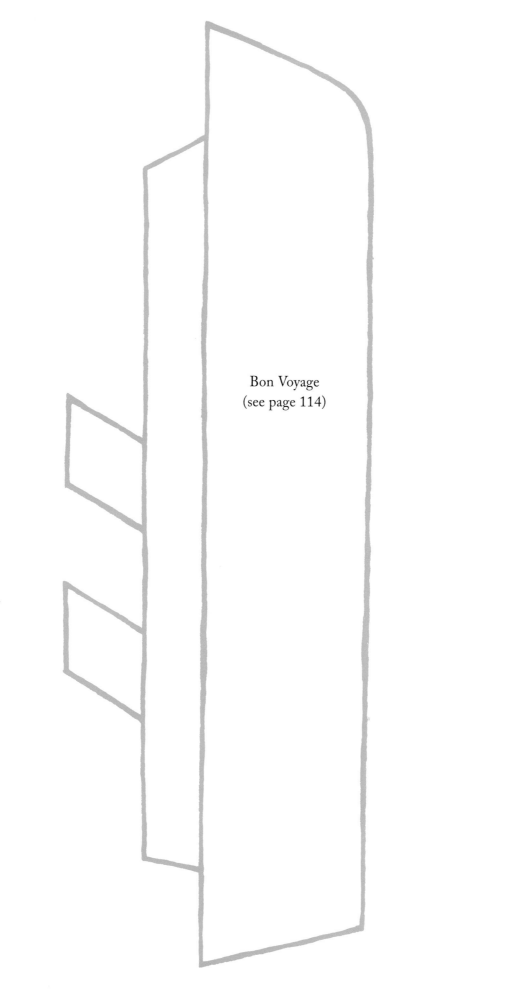

Bon Voyage
(see page 114)

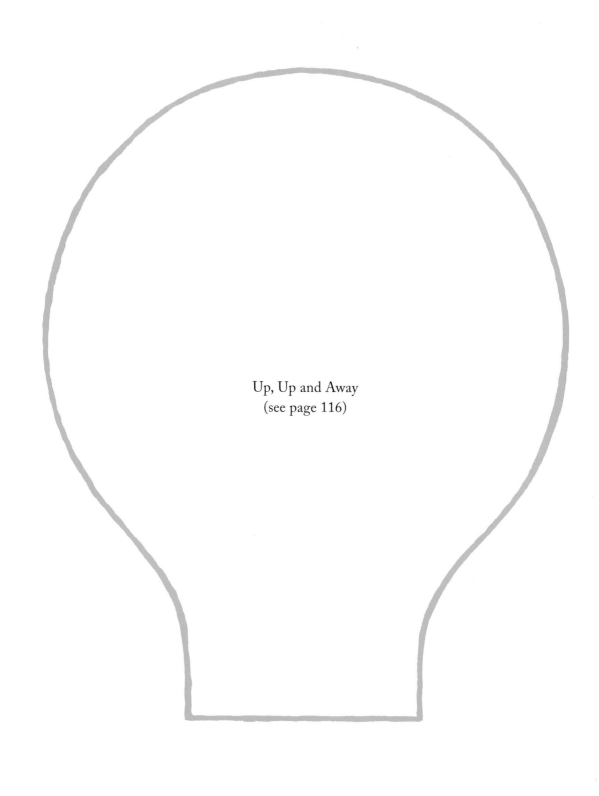

Up, Up and Away
(see page 116)

✻ *Acknowledgements* ✻

I would like to thank the following people who directly or indirectly have helped to put this book on the shelves:

My husband Ken, and children Kate and Emma. My parents, Mary and Mick Mallin and friends Janet and Roy Stevens for their permission to reproduce photographs. The Dough Designs team: Elizabeth Cook, Linda Allen, Debbie Vaughan, Victoria Cook, Pam Marchant and Sarah Day. Sue Bee of Susan Bee Jewellery and Joan Cobb of Cotswold Village Crafts. Rosemary Stammers for introducing me to doughcraft and Jane Greenoff for inspiring me to write. Finally, I would like to thank photographer Paul Biddle for his superb work, and everybody at David & Charles, for making the production of this book so enjoyable.

✻ *Further Reading* ✻

As there are now so many books on doughcraft available, it is not possible to list them all. The following are recommended:

Agate, Kristina, *Easy to Make Dough Crafts*, (Anaya, 1994)

Jones, Joanna, *Decorative Dough*, (Merehurst Ltd, 1993)

Kiskalt, Isolde, *Dough Crafts*, (Sterling/Lark, 1991)

Porteous, Brenda, *Fun Dough*, (David Porteous, 1992)

Rogers, Linda, *55 Country Doughcraft Designs*, (David & Charles 1994)